W9-BAJ-731

AN INTIMATE PORTRAIT
OF THE MAN BEHIND THE MINISTRY
IN *THE COMPASSIONATE TOUCH*

MARK

by Ron Hembree

Logos International
Plainfield, New Jersey

*This book is affectionately
dedicated to
Huldah,
Mark's lovely wife and
second in love only to his Lord.*

MARK
Copyright © 1979 by Logos International
All rights reserved
Printed in the United States of America
Library of Congress Catalog Card Number: 79-53495
International Standard Book Number: 0-88270-403-6
Logos International, Plainfield, New Jersey 07060

Preface

Special thanks to Mark Buntain for letting me write this book. The help of Doug Brendel, a brilliant young writer and close friend, has been inestimable. My deep appreciation also goes to my traveling companions, Dr. and Mrs. Al Holderness, my son, Rod, and my wife, Shirley. To Carol Adams, special thanks for her technical editing expertise, and Sue Seitz deserves volumes of gratitude for transcribing the tapes and for her many hours of typing.

But most of all, thank you for reading this work. My prayer is that your heart will be moved with compassion toward Mark and his ministry. He urgently needs our prayers and support. The greatest compliment I could ever receive from the readers of *Mark* is to know you have been moved to join the faithful prayer partners who daily lift this beloved missionary up to our Lord. Pray for India.

Ron Hembree

Contents

1

City of the Dreadful Night

Kali, the black and brooding Hindu goddess of death, hulks over the decaying city of Calcutta as its patron deity. It is an appropriate figure, since Kali, according to Hindu legend, is "the supreme night, which swallows all that exists."

She is portrayed as a lurking figure, laughing hideously as she dances on the prostrate body of the god Shiva. Kali dances with a raised sword in one of her four hands, a severed head in another.

No one who has ever visited this "city of the dreadful night" could ever deny that death dominates Calcutta with insidious glee.

Smell its fetid odor. Walk its filthy streets. Breathe its putrid air. Move among the living dead imprisoned here.

This is Calcutta. An outpost of hell.

"Calcutta assaults the senses like no other city on earth."* It is a city of disease and death, poverty and squalor. Even its few attempts at grandeur seem shabby in comparison with the rest of the world. Bloated like a decaying corpse, Calcutta jams over nine million inhabitants into its shantytowns, known as *bustees,* or its tiny apartments, or its garbage-littered streets. There are some less horrible parts of the city—and a few rich people—but even these fade quickly into the backdrop of squalid human deprivation.

Squatting sullenly on the Hooghly River, Calcutta sweats through the hot months, when the heat lies like a smelly blanket over the festering city. Monsoons flood the unkempt streets, scattering garbage and human excrement in a gooey sludge of disease through the muddy lanes where people build their pitiful shacks. The deadly sludge breeds epidemics, making Calcutta the cholera capital of the world. There always seems to be a plague of typhoid, cholera, or tetanus to keep the sloppy hospitals busy.

"Insects and undertakers," Macaulay wrote, "are

---

*This line is from a government brochure describing Calcutta. However, in the past few months several municipal officials are becoming deeply concerned about the plight of the city. They resent Calcutta being the "eyesore" of the world and are making strong attempts to clean up its filth.

the only living creatures which seem to enjoy the climate."

"I shall always be glad to have seen it," Winston Churchill wrote to his mother, "for the reason that it will be unnecessary for me to ever see it again."

Robert Clive called Calcutta the most wicked place in the universe. To Dom Moraes it was "spider city." Perhaps Rudyard Kipling described it best in his classic poem, "City of the Dreadful Night":

> Chance directed, chance erected, laid and built
> On the silt—
> Palace, byre, hovel—poverty and pride—
> Side by side;
> And, above the packed and pestilential town,
> Death looked down.

But a city is people, and it is here that the heartbreak of Calcutta is bared in ugly agony. The more than nine million residents of greater Calcutta occupy a land space of thirty-seven square miles—an area smaller than Little Rock, Arkansas, a small American city with only 185,000 inhabitants.

More than one-third of Calcutta's people live in *bustees*. These clusters of mud hovels or clapboard lean-tos are thrown up against any available standing wall. Sometimes they are stacked together in haphazard array.

Inside, a full-grown man can neither stand up nor lie down, and yet in many cases dozens of people live in the cramped quarters that should hold only two or three. Family members sleep in shifts—or out in the alleyways, exposed to the slashing rains and chilly nights.

But even the bustee resident is better off than the street dweller. Hundreds of thousands of displaced refugees live on Calcutta's open streets, where the open sewers spew their filth. They have literally no shelter whatsoever. They have come to Calcutta from the old war-torn Pakistan or from the outer reaches of India's countryside. There is no other place for them to live.

The street people own nothing but the clothing on their backs. They use any available doorstep or a stretch of open pavement as home, until the property owner has them driven off. Then they merely go down the street until they find another doorstep and set up housekeeping.

The street family prepares its meals on a small stove fueled by cow dung. They get water from filthy hydrants stuck carelessly on the streets. They have no privacy on the open street. Here they sleep, they eat, they make love, they eliminate body wastes, they die. The toilet is a wall or a railway crossing.

A wagon comes by daily to pick up the dead. The bodies are burned at nearby *ghats*, or crematoriums, and the ashes float down the Hooghly River, source of Calcutta's drinking water. Two-thirds of the city's water supply are without any form of filtration, although industrial and human wastes are also dumped directly into the rancid river. In Calcutta you never really know what—or whom—you are drinking.

Four out of five children in Calcutta must survive on less than nine hundred calories per day—about the substance of two Milky Way candy bars. A recent government report states that only 40 percent of Calcutta's population gets to eat more than one meal per day. The Indian government does not like to admit there is starvation in the country. They will tell you the grossly undernourished persons who die are victims of identifiable diseases. Oddly, however, those diseases which kill in Calcutta are cured in other parts of the world through simple nutritional measures. The vast majority of these hopeless masses have dysentery, and the open sewers are cesspools of sickness. Most of the street people and bustee dwellers run continuous fevers because of infections.

Calcutta is also a city of hopeless traffic bottlenecks, with streets that have not been repaired in years. In fact, no more than five miles of major new roads have been added in the last twenty years. There are no highway trucks or equipment. All paving is done by hand. On any given day, from one-third to two-thirds of the city's ancient buses, trams, garbage trucks, and ambulances are out of order. Moving through Calcutta's traffic is like trying to solve some complicated riddle.

Hospitals in the city are horribly overcrowded,

with six thousand people to every available hospital bed. Hospital conditions are deplorable. Just a few months ago, rats chewed away the head of a newborn baby in one of Calcutta's major hospitals. Since then, the hospital has asked all patients to bring cats with them to protect them from the rats. The cats are kept busy: for each human being in Calcutta, there are eight rats—seventy-two million in all, and each one carrying disease.

Sanitation is virtually unknown. There are forty thousand open privies in the city. These are prime breeding grounds for flies, and they flush directly into the streets.

There are few brick and pipe sewers and these are usually clogged. The only method of clearing them is by lowering small children (called gully pit boys) into the manholes and having them shovel out the sludge with bare hands.

Before World War II there was one major garbage incinerator in Calcutta—but the British put it out of commission as a civil defense measure, afraid the furnace would attract Japanese bombers. It was never replaced or restored.

But Calcutta does have the world's cleanest garbage. Forty thousand ragpickers see to this. These are part of the desperate poor who scavenge through the city's garbage looking for a scrap of food or piece of cloth. They rarely find food, but they are happy to eat it when they do. They also pick out the rags and discarded tin cans to make second-generation junk products, which they sell to keep themselves alive. Although there is a major dump at the edge of the city, there is no incentive for hauling the waste there, for garbage is piled indiscriminately in Calcutta's streets.

Perhaps most damaging to the Indians' human dignity is Calcutta's desperate unemployment. Joseph Lelyveld, who politely describes Calcutta's problem as "underemployment," says, "The con men and beggars are but the most startling and visible of vast legions who have no hope of regular employment and so must invent livelihoods for themselves out of nothing in order to survive."

He goes on to explain that every dilapidated taxi in Calcutta has two men riding in front. One is the driver, and the other is employed to put down the flag on the meter and keep the driver company. In reality, however, every taxi has a crew of four to six; every vehicle is used twenty-four hours a day, so as many as possible can eke out a living from it. There are also 368 drivers for the 110 city lorries assigned to the city conservancy department.

Similarly, there are four rickshaw pullers for every rickshaw. Each one is straining to earn a few rupees per day (rarely more than forty American cents). From this he has to pay the *bara babu* who owns the rickshaw. But to reach five-and-a-half rupees per day on a nine-hour shift, the puller has to haul ten to twenty fares—totaling at least seven or eight miles—padding barefoot through streets that are either broiling or flooded. One might expect the pullers to grow muscular through exercise, but lack of nutrition keeps them universally emaciated and weak.

Still, the rickshaw puller has an easy life compared to some of Calcutta's other "underemployed." Thousands of fathers compete with animals for jobs to support their families. They pull carts, push heavy loads, drag barges up the river by tugging on long ropes from the banks. Basement excavations are done by hand, with teams of men pulling heavy scrapers that dig out the dirt. To drive piles for building foundations, scores of men pull up a heavy weight with ropes and pullies, letting it drop onto a steel shaft. The men of Calcutta will carry, push, or pull anything just to earn a few rupees to buy a bowl of rice.

Nowhere else in the world can you find as many sidewalk hawkers. They are the world's most persistent—and most desperate—salesmen. The hawkers and their families make toys out of tin cans, works of art out of rags, or anything that might bring a rupee or two.

Prostitution is epidemic. A recent survey indicated it was the second most common occupation among Calcutta's women. Only housewives outnumber them.

Thousands sell cow dung for a living. Dung is used as fuel in the little stoves that dot the city streets and bustees. The cow dung salesman pays two rupees per cow to the owner for all the dung it can produce in a day. Then he mixes the dung with sawdust or straw and pats it out into pancakes to dry. The dung can be seen on almost every wall or pole in Calcutta, drying in the tropical sun, and the smell of the fresh cow dung crowns the sickening stench of the city.

The despair of unemployment is felt most deeply by the youth. Recently the Indian government announced it was creating 17,000 make-work jobs. Nearly one-and-a-half-million people applied for these jobs. An insider at one private corporation says when they put a single classified ad in the newspaper for a job opening, 5,000 will apply if experience is required; 10,000 if no experience is required. There is little laziness—rather, Calcutta's youth are consumed with a drive to become valuable. Every day sacks of mail with job applications are delivered to major industries. Most stores sell manuals on how to write letters to prospective employers. Hundreds of thousands of young people faithfully copy these letters and send them to employers. But they seldom hear back. On the steps of the General Post Office you can buy certificates of attendance at Calcutta University. Applications for jobs at various corporations sell for two or three cents each, and the printers make big profits on them.

Since India has no regular welfare program, the elderly and sick must be cared for by family members. This is why birth control is an absurd concept for the Indian. By limiting his family, he cuts off the only security he has when he gets sick and old. The family burden is a hard one to carry. Young people are generally forbidden to marry and form their own family until their obligations to parents are taken care of. During a visit to Calcutta, my wife met a beautiful twenty-six-year-old Indian girl. She suggested, "Let me pray with you that you will find a loving husband."

The girl sighed, "It won't do any good because I can't marry. I must support my mother, brothers and sisters." She felt hopelessly locked into a life of loneliness.

One authority noted recently that a good education does not assure a future for the Calcutta youth. "Examination results mean less than nothing," he says. In recent years university authorities have systematically lowered standards in Calcutta in order to make sure their graduates are at no disadvantage in competing for jobs with students from the rest of India. When exams are held, the proctors who are supposed to prevent cheating are threatened with physical violence if they dare to try. Routinely, most of them collect five rupees (about seventy cents) from each student as a fee for looking away. New questions are rarely posed, for then it would be impossible to locate the answers in the "bazaar notes." Some of these grotesquely irrelevant, embalmed specimens of British pedagogy are probably a century old: "Indicate the theme of the poem, 'The Lady of Shalott,' and expound its symbolical meaning or significance." It is natural to wonder what the question and poem could mean to a student who has enough English to follow them, but that leaves out the overwhelming majority.

It is little wonder that employers in the face of such frustration rely on family connections or "caste" to determine who they employ. An applicant from a "respectable family" with a good recommendation from a well-established businessman or high-ranking civil servant always has a tremendous edge. Over two-thirds of those employed found their work through "connections." Such a system keeps both the poor and the rich locked in their places. Thus, thousands of hopeless youth wander the streets trying to pick up odd jobs. At one hotel where I stayed, there were five waiters for every table. One brought the water, another the salad. A third took care of the bread. The fourth delivered the main course and dessert. The fifth brought the bill. Waiting on tables is a preferred position in Calcutta—for waiters have first choice of whatever their customers leave on the plate. The young people have no hope, and they know it. But only the outsider can sense the magnitude of Calcutta's total wasted human potential.

In such a society, it is little wonder that begging is a major industry. Professional beggars gross the equivalent of ten million dollars per year. There is even a beggar caste in India. Children of the rank are taught early in life how to elicit sympathy. There are estimated to be nearly 200,000 professional beggars in Calcutta, over half of whom have gross physical disabilities. In fact, it is well known that many beggars break the arms and legs of their children to make them cripples. Crippled children get more sympathy—and more rupees.

Competing with the professional beggar is the genuine one—the hollow-eyed, gaunt-cheeked Indian without family or friend who desperately needs a bowl of rice. Walking the streets of Calcutta, it is difficult to distinguish between the desperately needy and the slick actor-beggars. Both types gather at every marketplace. They meet you at the airport. They surround the hotel. There is hardly a place in Calcutta where you can escape their haunting eyes and outstretched hands.

The despair of Calcutta is summed up in one of its poet's bitter wishes: Rabindranath Tagore, the great Bengali poet, laments, "If there is rebirth, may I not be born in Bengal again." It is common for pastors of the city to hear their hospitalized parishioners cry, "Oh, pastor, please pray that I will die." Not long ago a group of British and American urban experts traveled to Calcutta. They left shaking their heads. Their report: They had never seen human degradation on a comparable scale in any other city of the world.

I shall never forget my first trip to Calcutta. Traveling with me were my wife, my son, a doctor, and his wife. As we were driven from the airport into the entrails of the filthy, fetid city, we were swallowed by the sights and sounds and smells. We passed tiny children with bloated bellies suffering from malnutrition, hollow-eyed mothers and bony fathers shuffling through the bowels of the city.

As we drove, I watched the reactions on the faces of my traveling companions. Dr. Al Holderness grew red-faced, and his eyes flashed with anger at the filth and carelessness. He could almost see the epidemics sweeping the city. All this sickness, he knew, would be unnecessary with proper hygiene.

The doctor's wife, Jan, was nervously chatting, talking in illogical circles. Her voice squeaked higher and higher as the city overwhelmed us. But she talked on, desperately trying to verbally erase the scenes of sorrow unfolding in front of her eyes.

My son, sixteen years old, sat in stunned silence. His eyes were wide with fear. Somehow his young mind could not absorb and comprehend such an existence in any human setting.

And then I looked at my wife. She sat motionless, with great tears washing down her face.

Many in our world have given up on Calcutta. Some experts predict it cannot survive the next decade. They claim some cataclysmic disaster will occur soon, although it is difficult to imagine anything more horrible than what is happening now. They say conditions are simply too despairing, that Calcutta is ripe for a massive disaster that will wipe it

13

out entirely.

Most recoil in horror or flee in confusion from this place. For if Calcutta is not hell, it is certainly hell's front porch.

But there is a man who has not given up on Calcutta. He has marched on this outpost of hell to reclaim it for the human family. In a city of Satan, he is a saint.

He is no Johnny-come-lately, however. For over a quarter of a century, Mark Buntain has lived in Calcutta. He has filled his lungs with its putrid air. He has muddied his shoes in the streets. His once crystal clear announcer's voice is now but a hoarse whisper from years of preaching in its polluted air.

But moreover, he has embraced Calcutta as his own. He has reached into this cesspool of humanity to redeem the dying.

He has no time for those who curse the darkness. Instead, he has lit a candle.

He is a gentle man, and yet he is shaking his fist in the face of Satan. He has wrenched precious lives from the grasp of hell.

Instead of looking at the city as it stands and asking "Why?", he has looked at it as it should be, asking "Why not?" He searches the streets of Calcutta for the wounded and wanting. He is Calcutta's angel of mercy.

With a calm resoluteness, he has hung a light on the front porch of hell.

And this is Mark Buntain's story.

2

Too Deep for Comfort

The dark-eyed little girl pulls urgently on the white missionary's large hand.

"Come with me. Please, sahib."

Mark Buntain looks down at her with a face full of love and warmth—a round face, soft and open, with eyeglasses hooked over slightly large ears. He is clearly a human being—not an Apollo.

He follows the hollow-cheeked, ragged child down a muddy bustee lane, toward one of the little shanties. Mark stands taller than most Indians, and his clean clothes and white skin make him all the more unusual. But nobody reads pride into his appearance. Instead, the message is loving. "There is hope. Let me help."

When they arrive at the little girl's hut, Mark

steps over the sludge of the sewer to get to the doorway. He must stoop to enter.

It is pitch-black inside. As his eyes adjust to the darkness, Mark sees a young woman lying on a filthy cot, barely breathing. She hardly turns her head to look at the strange white man.

"I have come to help you," Mark says. "Where is your husband?"

"Oh, sahib," she whispers hoarsely, "when he found out I had leprosy, he left us. The only way we eat is when my father gets odd jobs and a little money. Otherwise, we just have to wait."

Within a few minutes the sick woman's father arrives, and Mark draws the tired old Indian aside.

"This evening we have a service at our church," he tells the old man. "Would you come? And tomorrow morning, if you'll come to our hospital, I will give you some medicine and start treatment for your daughter's leprosy."

Early the next morning the old Indian arrives at the hospital in the heart of Calcutta. Doctors give him the medicine, set up a treatment schedule for his daughter, and give him food for the family. The care-worn wrinkles of the old man's face smooth into a faint smile.

Leaving Mark and the hospital that morning, he turns to the strange white man, clutches the precious medicine and food as if it might evaporate, and says, "Sahib, you don't know how good it feels to know that someone cares."

Mark Buntain does care. In fact, he cares so deeply that his friends despair for his health. He has thrown the energies of his life into the havoc of Calcutta—touching, lifting, and loving the poorest of the poor in our world's most hopeless city.

That caring is unstoppable—almost an entity in itself that consumes Mark Buntain night and day. It drives him to push his body and mind to their natural limits—and then some. It has driven him like this, in fact, for a quarter of a century.

Every other talent or ambition or goal that Mark might have had along the way—any other life he might have lived—all of this has been shunted aside.

For none of these is India. Mark has had other opportunities. The offers have come and gone, and come again. Wealth and power and a certain amount of easy fame have been offered.

But they are always rejected. They are not India. And India is Mark's to love. He must press on, loving India, feeding Calcutta, binding the wounds, rebuilding the bodies, salvaging souls.

For those he has not yet reached, he weeps. For the thousands who still die hungry, his heart aches. Mention the need that Calcutta represents, and Mark Buntain's eyes brim over with tears. He loves too deeply for comfort.

On one of his trips to the United States—trips which are necessary to raise money for the work in India—Mark was invited to the home of a pastor in the Midwest. After dinner, Mark and his hosts retired to the living room. The pastor had thoughtfully obtained an album of Indian music.

One of the songs on the record was the haunting "Song of India." Mark was captivated by its music. He asked to hear the piece again, and again, and then again.

He was transfixed. After a couple hours of this monotony, the pastor and his family finally gave up on all attempts at conversation, leaving the missionary absorbed in the music.

Deep in the night, the pastor awoke and looked at his clock. It was two o'clock, and he could still hear the music playing.

Wrapping his robe about him, the pastor tiptoed to the living room. There was Mark, lying on his back on the floor. Tears washed down his cheeks. Hoarse from hours of intercession, he was still whispering over and over, "India, my India—Jesus, please save India."

The pastor slipped quietly back to bed. He still does not know how many more hours Mark prayed for his beloved country and its dying people before finally dropping off to sleep.

But it is one thing to weep over the plight of a people, and quite another to take action to relieve human suffering. Mark has done—and is doing—both. The tears flowing from his breaking heart all these years have been transformed to seed, and from the seed has sprung one of the most remarkable and miraculous stories of our century.

Only within the recent past has anyone even attempted to tell the story. It still sounds so incredible that skeptics wonder if it could be true.

But it is true. It seems God loved Calcutta so much that He prepared a very special vessel to carry His love to the city. During the two-and-a-half decades Mark has been in India, he has built a modern, six-story hospital, containing some of the world's finest and most modern equipment. Today, even Indian government officials prefer Mark's hospital when they become ill or their children need care.

It was a ministry dictated by need—and compassion.

Mark and Huldah found thousands in Calcutta who were in desperate need of medical treatment but had no place to go—and no money with which to pay. A few years ago, for example, a young couple begged Mark to help them find a hospital bed for their sick infant.

"We have an emergency case," Mark told the nurse in the pediatric ward of a government hospital, hoping they might have room. "Would you please give me a bed for this little baby? I suspect she is dying."

The nurse waved her hands in the air, irritated by Mark's concern.

"They're all dying," she replied, "What makes this child any different than the others?"

It was true. People were dying everywhere. This

couple was only representative of thousands of others.

Mark's spirit began to burn with a desire to build a hospital which would be open to everyone—even those who could not pay.

Mark also pastors a church with 2,500 members. There are services in six languages each Sunday. It is the first major church to be erected in Calcutta in the last one hundred years. (A Seventh Day Adventist church is the only other assembly ever attempted in the last century.)

Today Mark's church is bursting at the seams. This has prompted a further expansion program. Evangelist Jimmy Swaggart is helping Mark build a new and larger evangelistic center to handle the expanding work. After Jimmy Swaggart visited Mark's work in Calcutta, seeing the great need that exists there, he decided to supply additional funds to assist in the feeding of 7,000 children daily. He also pledged additional large grants for future needs.

Mark also conducts an international radio broadcast, beaming the gospel message from his church to touch thousands of lives in other parts of Asia. He has started scores of satellite churches and supervises over forty village congregations as well.

Mark also feeds seven thousand starving children every day, which has made him a legend in humanitarian circles. The feeding program grew out of a miniature tragedy that occurred before Mark's eyes. A little girl in his school was asked to read her lesson aloud. As she stood, she collapsed to the floor.

"Honey, what did you have for breakfast this morning?" Mark asked her after she was revived.

She looked down, embarrassed.

"Nothing, sir."

"What did you have last night?" he asked gently.

"Nothing, sir."

"How about for breakfast yesterday morning?" Mark persisted.

"*Poree*," she replied. Poree is a flour pastry fried in oil. The girl had fallen unconscious from hunger.

And she was only one of thousands in the same situation. Mark realized the children of Calcutta had a desperate need for food to make them strong—strong enough to combat the tuberculosis, typhoid, cholera, and smallpox that ravage the city with its scant water supply and poor sanitation.

In that moment, Mark seized on the story of the loaves and the fishes and determined to feed the children of Calcutta by the power of God. Since then he has been able to give meals to more than three million children through his daily feeding program.

Mark also has a highly approved and fully accredited school for 2,500 Indian children. An additional 1,500 attend village schools he has started around Calcutta.

He operates a drug center for troubled youth.

He has conceived and nurtured scores of village churches and treatment centers, all the way from Calcutta to the border of Bangladesh.

He has a sophisticated school for nurses and a mobile hospital that travels to the bustees every week.

He has a major printing plant which produces Christian literature to be distributed throughout Calcutta. Over 200,000 are enrolled in his Bible correspondence courses.

And between the hospital, the feeding kitchen, the printing plants, and the schools, Mark's ministry is a major industry, employing over five hundred Indians.

Each difficult piece of the work has been built by the sweat of Mark's brow and the tenacity of his faith. Caring costs. He lives every moment in the realm of compassion.

Once, fifteen miles south of Calcutta, Mark spied a young boy hobbling down a dirt road on double clubbed feet. His feet were so twisted that the tops of his feet were really the bottoms. Mark only needed one look at the boy to know that the doctors could help him.

A crowd gathered around the missionary as he examined the lad. Among them was the boy's father.

"Sir, please let me have your little boy," Mark asked. "I know God will help us straighten his feet."

"But we just don't have the money, sir," he replied.

"You don't need the money; just bring the boy," Mark told him.

They kept the crippled child at the hospital for

several months, to build him up physically so he could withstand the anesthetic necessary for an operation. After several operations, the lad's feet were straightened. Not long after that, the whole staff gathered on the hospital steps to watch the little fellow walk to his daddy, as normal as anyone.

Sometimes people, regardless of their terrible plight, resent intrusion from "outsiders." In fact, embassy officials of India often tell Westerners, "The Indian people are happy; don't disturb them with Western culture.

But those words are public relations ploys. The sick, desperate and starving ones—who have to live in the squalor and pain—feel differently. There is great love and admiration for those like Mother Teresa, who operates an orphanage, and Mark Buntain. Most often the average Indian does not understand why a man like Mark will do what he does. The Indian's religions and culture are contrary to the "brother's keeper" concept.

Basically the Indian religions teach men to turn inward for inner peace, escaping the hell of their lives by introspection. They say, "Get in touch with yourself." Christianity teaches just the opposite, saying a relationship with God is two-dimensional: I must love my Lord and love my neighbor as myself. Jesus teaches that people are to get in touch with God and each other. That is why Mark often declares, "Nobody cares outside of Jesus." It is true; only those who know and love Jesus Christ really care about the open sores of our wounded world.

Perhaps the best example of how the Indian feels about Mark and his remarkable ministry is summed up by one Indian nonbeliever. He was being interviewed by Doug Wead for the bestseller, *The Compassionate Touch*. "I have seen Jesus," the old man said to Wead. "He is not in America."

The wrinkled, emaciated old man smiled a toothless smile and pointed his bony finger in the author's face.

"When the children come for their food in the morning and see that Pastor Buntain is there, and they dip the milk, you can see Jesus."

The Indian's smile widened.

"You go out there tomorrow morning and watch. You too can see Jesus there."

Doug Wead speaks in reverence about Mark Buntain. In *The Compassionate Touch* he writes that Mark is a mysterious and provocative man. "He has appeared out of nowhere, a phantom angel to thousands of homeless children and crippled beggars. He feeds them like a lover of nature would feed hungry birds. He sets their crippled wings, and when they are able, lets them fly freely away. Yet always they return to him."

It is true. There are many who have been helped by Mark and have vowed to spend the rest of their lives working for him. Even if they come, receive help, and wander away, they always come back. Mark is like a great magnet, always drawing the ones whose lives he has touched, no matter where they might stray.

Trying to explain Mark and his ministry, Wead says, "I think it is not so much what he *does* as what he *is* that makes Mark Buntain a truly great man of God. It is his character, his integrity, and most of all his compassion."

But how does a man do so much with so little? How can a human being live in the sewer and yet see the roses? How can you spend twenty-five years in hell and still have the glow of heaven?

The answers are not easy to come by. However, when one looks at the life of Mark Buntain, it is strangely reminiscent of God's reminder to Jeremiah centuries ago. "Before I formed thee in the belly I knew thee; and before thou camest forth out of the womb I sanctified thee, and I ordained thee a prophet unto the nations" (Jer. 1:5).

Mark loves to quote David Livingstone, the famed missionary to Africa. When someone asked Livingstone how he could bring himself to sacrifice his entire life for missions in Africa, the missionary replied, "Sir, if a commission by an earthly king be considered an honor, how can a commission by a heavenly king be considered a sacrifice?"

"Little did I know," Mark says, "that when I was growing up in Winnipeg, Canada, I would have *the joy* of being used of God to show the slum-dwellers of Calcutta how much Jesus loves them."

Oddly, though, that youngster who came out of

the plains of Canada had very little in common with the Mark Buntain who came to weep for India.

. Mark wanted to preach as a young man but he resisted God's timing. And yet, when he finally submitted, God blessed him beautifully.

He resisted when the Holy Spirit was being poured out in his life, and yet giving in to that infilling gave him a new power and a new perspective.

He balked when he was assigned his first pastorate. And yet when he finally gave in, God used those years to mature him.

At each stop along the way, God was preparing him for a rare and trying ministry. At each stop, Mark had to learn great, difficult lessons of faith—and submission—before he could go on.

God was preparing Mark Buntain for the toughest step of all—the call to India. It seems impossible but, even from the beginning, the call to India was a thing Mark despised.

He had taken a wife—Huldah, the daughter of missionaries to Japan—and they now had a baby girl named Bonnie. The three Buntains had moved on to the evangelistic circuit. Life became more and more comfortable as the crowds flocked to the meetings Mark held across the North American continent.

But Mark knew—from God's past dealings with him—that he must always continue to seek the Father's perfect will for his life. And the searching in Mark's heart—like a compass needle, swinging ever northward—eventually led the young evangelist to sense that change was coming.

There was something else God wanted him to do.

That change finally came into focus at Kelso, Washington. Mark took time from his own meetings to attend a missionary convention featuring John Hall, a retired missionary to Africa. Mark stood at the back of the auditorium since there were no seats available.

The message was moving, and Mark felt a deep tug on his heart. When Rev. Hall called for commitments from the congregation, Mark was one of the first to step forward.

"At that moment, I knew God was calling me to the mission field," Mark says. "I also knew God was speaking to Huldah. God had some yet unknown to us—but great—plan for our lives."

Mark felt no resistance to the missionary call. The resistance—the heartache—still lay ahead.

Within a few weeks Mark was invited to hold revival meetings throughout the Orient. The meetings were tremendously successful, but at each stop Mark found himself challenged to stay as a missionary.

As he prepared to leave the Tokyo airport, one of the missionaries to Japan pulled Mark aside and said, "Mark, we need you and Huldah here. Your mother-in-law and father-in-law were pioneer missionaries in this country. They built the first pentecostal church of Japan. Please come back and help us."

It was tempting to say yes. Huldah could relate easily to this mission field. And Mark felt comfortable in Japan.

But Mark had learned by now that he was not the master of his own destiny. So he replied, "Brother, I will, if our Lord lets me."

At that moment an inner voice spoke to Mark, *You will go to India*.

Mark turned cold.

"No, Lord. No," he began to pray fervently, "anywhere but India."

He had heard the horror stories. He had no desire to be a hero—or a martyr.

"I don't want to go to India," he prayed desperately.

Shaken by the encounter, he said nothing to Huldah.

A few weeks later, a representative of the Assemblies of God foreign missions department called Mark. Would he accept an assignment in Taipei in China? Mark had effectively preached to great crowds of Chinese during his trip to the Orient.

"I will go," Mark told the man, "if the Lord lets me."

It was difficult to be so casual. Mark had felt for years that he would someday preach in China—ever since he had experienced a vision at a camp meeting as a young man. In the vision, he saw himself preaching to mammoth crowds of Chinese people.

But again, that strong, inner voice echoed the awful prophecy, *You will go to India.*

Again Mark recoiled.

"No! No, Lord! I don't want to go to India!"

Again he said nothing to Huldah.

Shortly thereafter, Mark was preaching for his father in Edmonton, Alberta, when he received an urgent letter from the missions department of the Assemblies of God.

"Would you proceed immediately to Calcutta, India?" the letter asked. "We desperately need you there."

Dad Buntain was standing in the parlor of the parsonage when Mark handed the letter to him. The elder Buntain read it silently. Mark knew God was leading him to India, and his godly father felt the same leading. It was cord-cutting time.

"Mark," he said quietly, "you had better go."

3

Stay, Go, Stop, Proceed

Huldah was playing with baby Bonnie on the bed when Mark received the letter. They had waited nine years for their daughter, and she seemed like a special blessing from heaven—the greatest joy of her parents' lives.

Now Mark walked grimly into the bedroom and handed Huldah the letter.

Huldah's eyes raced over the page and then burst into tears. "Oh, Mark, I'll go anywhere," she cried, anguished. "But please don't ask me to take my baby to India!"

Mark soothed her and told her how God had been dealing with his heart. Huldah understood.

Soon they were selling the few things they had accumulated. As each piece was carried away,

Huldah struggled to keep her composure.

A long list of items arrived from the missions department. They were things considered necessary for survival in Calcutta. Huldah sadly began shopping. They would leave for India.

They were tight-lipped days, tense and quiet.

But Mark was obeying the voice of God in spite of his feelings of doubt, and God honored his obedience. When Mark and Huldah went to Vancouver to her sister's home to say good-bye, one of the family friends called Mark outside onto the lawn.

"Mark, if your mother-in-law has her fare paid for, would you like her to go with you to India?"

Mark could hardly believe what he was hearing. His father-in-law had died years before. Huldah's mother had often traveled with them on the evangelistic field. She was a great prayer warrior and helped out with the music. It would be a joy for her to go, but most of all it would ease the pressure on Huldah with the baby.

"I'll pay her passage," the friend said.

Mark rejoiced in God's provision.

But there were still thousands of miles to be covered. And no great step is taken for God without the enemy of the soul trying to interfere. From the beginning it seemed as if Satan was determined to make sure the Buntains would never make it to Calcutta.

They arrived in New York and had to wait for

passage. They stayed in a large home in the Bronx where missionaries from various missions boards gathered to wait for ships.

While they waited, Mark received a telegram from the Indian field secretary of the missions board.

"Do not go to India," it ordered tersely. "Plans have been changed."

Mark couldn't understand what this was all about. He phoned the headquarters office to hear the explanation.

"Well, Mark, there have been some difficulties out there," the executive said. "Now the difficulties have been resolved. It seems we don't need you there any more."

"Brother, God doesn't change His mind that quickly," Mark replied. As little as he wanted to go to India, Mark still knew God's call had been genuine.

"I'll tell you, Mark," the missionary replied, having been put on the spot. "We do need an *evangelist* in India. Why don't you go to India for one year and then come home?"

This decision would be crucial in the difficult days ahead.

Five days later the Buntains boarded ship for London, where they got on board another boat to Calcutta.

London could not have been worse. The air was damp and cold. Once again the Buntains had to stay at one of the missionary houses. Food was scarce and the house sat far from the city or any shopping center.

To make matters worse, the Buntains couldn't get boat passage to India. No one had any room for the missionaries on their ships. Tourists and sightseers had booked all the available spaces. There was nothing to do but wait and endure the bleakness of old England.

After a few weeks of miserable living Mark had waited long enough. He took his family to the Thomas Cooke Company in London, the shipping concern which was slated to book passage for the Buntains. He was determined to apply some pressure.

"Rev. Buntain, please don't come back again," the general manager told him. "There is not a passage on any boat. We know where you are staying and we have your telephone number. When we have any room, we will let you know."

Mark dragged his disappointed family all the way back to the missionary home.

When they walked into the house, Mark followed his mother-in-law to her room. "Mother, Jesus said if two will agree touching anything we ask of our Father in heaven, He will give it to us," he said resolutely. "Will you agree with me right now in prayer that we will get passage on a boat?"

They only prayed for a few short moments, but Mark knew God was already at work. No sooner had they spoken the prayer than Mark left the house and boarded a bus back to the Thomas Cooke Company.

When he walked in the front door, the shipping manager bumped into him. "Mr. Buntain, I was just on my way to phone you," he said with a surprised look. "We have found passage on a brand-new Dutch vessel. It's making its maiden voyage from Amsterdam to Djakarta, Indonesia. They just told me there is room for three people and they will stop near Calcutta. Hurry and get your things ready. You leave tomorrow."

God was still at work.

Finally the Buntains were on their way.

But the crossing was difficult. All of the passengers and crew were Dutchmen and only one young lady spoke passable English. The Buntains felt isolated from the world.

The language gap drove them to their books—perhaps the most redeeming part of the trip. During the voyage Mark read a biography of the apostle Paul—something which would have a tremendous impact on his life for years to come. As the boat made its way through the Mediterranean Sea, Mark sat on the deck and traced the footsteps of Paul.

When the boat touched the shores of North Africa, the Buntains were able to get off board for a few hours. Then there was that long and dreadful trip through the Suez Canal—a war zone filled with tension and danger. The Buntains had quarters down in the bowels of the boat. It was excruciatingly hot, and they were not able to open the porthole for fear water would spill over into the vessel. At times it seemed as though they would not make it.

When the exhausted Buntains finally arrived in India, a missionary met them and delivered three letters that had come for Mark. One was from the missionary superintendent for South India. It said, "Don't go to Calcutta; stay in South India."

The second letter, from the North India superintendent, said, "Don't stay in the south; come to North India."

The third came from the field secretary for the entire nation of India. "Proceed to Calcutta," the letter advised.

Mark didn't know what to do, so he looked at the postmarks and followed the advice of the earliest letter, trusting God's prompting. It was the Calcutta directive.

It would take another week on a boat to get up river to Calcutta. The three Buntains were anxious to be done with water travel, so they arranged to get on the first available boat. Perhaps soon they could rest, they thought. Once they finally got settled, they imagined, things would seem a little better.

But disaster was pursuing them.

Just as Mark and his family started to board their boat for Calcutta, a messenger came running with a fresh cable. Mark stood in stunned silence, the paper hanging limp from his hand.

"Dad very ill," the cable read. "Full of cancer. Pray. Mom."

Mark could hardly believe the message. He

reached back in his mind for a picture of his father's last handshake, only weeks before. It was firm as ever. Was he sick then? Mark could not recall any complaint of pain. Dad had seemed a little weary, perhaps, but that was all. He had certainly seemed healthy.

But now—"Full of cancer. Pray."

Mark felt the sting of tears in his eyes, and he shut them tight. He clamped his teeth together and began to follow his mother's order: "Pray."

It was all he could do. His dad was half a world away, and Mark had to proceed to Calcutta.

Numbed, the little missionary family boarded the S.S. *City of Madras* for the week-long voyage up the Hooghly River to Calcutta.

They longed for a place to call home. They needed to rest and feel secure. They hoped to find a little peace in the city of their calling.

But the first sight of Calcutta slapped them sharply in the face. It was wretched and ugly.

"Everywhere I looked," Mark recalls, "I could only see death and dejection. It seemed as if all were suffering and sick."

His heart was moved with compassion, but he also was sick with disgust. His proper Canadian upbringing had made him a tidy person. Here, he was assaulted by the disease and disorder that was "The City of the Dreadful Night."

"When we ate our first lunch in India," Mark remembers, "I sat at the table with tears trickling down my face. My wife said, 'What's wrong?' I didn't answer her. But the truth was—I just didn't want to be there."

Mark Buntain hated India, and especially Calcutta. A great battle was going on inside of him. He was in culture shock. He had brought his family to a great, awful pit. He was angry and hurt.

On the third day in Calcutta, another cable arrived from Mark's mother.

"Dad is dying. Please come home."

Mark stood, tortured, clutching the cable in his hand, tears streaming down his face. The questions seared his mind. Had he made a mistake? Should he have come to this city he hated? Was he too impulsive? Did he miss God's will when he ignored the letter in New York? Was he really needed at all in this God-forsaken hole?

Now his dad was dying. Now he must leave his wife and baby in an alien culture to fend for themselves—for how long, no one could say.

His world was coming apart.

Tormented, he went to the airport to talk with someone from British Airways. He had no money and knew no one in the city except two missionary couples. After breathing a word of prayer, Mark walked up to the first counter and laid out his predicament.

"If you will trust me for the fare," Mark told the agent, "I promise I will pay it back to you as soon as I get home to Canada."

But God was still in control of Mark's shattered life. It was no accident that he was talking to this particular ticket agent.

"Sir, I am a Christian," the young man replied. "You are not to worry. We will take care of you."

The agent booked Mark on the last seat available. He made out a ticket and then stamped a word across the front of it: COMPASSIONATE.

Even in his confusion and sorrow, Mark knew his loving Lord was still with him.

Mark situated Huldah, her mother, and the baby in a missionary's home; they promised Mark they would be all right. He was not sure. Where would the tragedies end?

As the old four-engined propeller plane churned its way slowly through the sky, Mark's mind drifted forward to his father's bedside, where the rest of the family would already be gathered around the stricken figure. But, inevitably, his mind drifted backward in time, to scenes of his beloved father in healthier, happier times.

4

Defrocked

They were a blend of Scottish and English, those Buntains, having migrated to central Canada generations before. Mark's father, Daniel Newton Buntain, finished college and went to the wilds of Saskatchewan to teach school. His plan was to earn enough money to attend a Methodist seminary and become a preacher.

Determined to make good on the vast plains of Canada's breadbasket, Dan Buntain soon learned Saskatchewan's scattered schools were many miles apart and hard for farm children to reach. To remedy that problem, the young and innovative school teacher set up a simple system for busing the children. This started the first consolidated school system in Canada. Because of his outstanding organizational ability, Dan was made principal of the school. With the growing system, he soon found himself in need of additional teachers.

The prairie province of Saskatchewan is sparsely populated, so young Buntain was forced to obtain his teachers from the more populous area of Canada. He advertised for teachers in the *Toronto Star*, Canada's largest newspaper.

The ad fell into the hands of a young English girl who lived with her family in Belleville, Ontario. She had just finished college and wanted to be a missionary to Japan, but she had to teach until she could make enough money to attend the Women's Methodist Training School in Toronto. When she read the ad, she immediately wrote to Saskatchewan, sending Dan Buntain her meager resume and college transcripts.

Although the Baileys were reluctant to see their daughter, Kathleen, go as far west as Saskatchewan, they understood her deep desire to become a missionary. They were old-fashioned Methodists and wanted their children in the service of God. They agreed she should take the job in Saskatchewan.

Dan Buntain wired Kathleen. At their first interview he was more impressed by her charm than her credentials, and he timidly asked her to dinner. They had not worked together long before they began to talk about their mutual desire for the ministry. Slowly but surely their love bloomed. Dan proposed and Kathleen accepted. Within a few months the marriage took place, and Kathleen decided if she could not go to Japan as a missionary, she would give all her energies to helping her husband become a minister, and together they would raise their children to serve the Lord. Perhaps one of the children could be a missionary, she mused.

The young couple moved back to eastern Canada, and Dan finished his training for the ministry. He was finally ordained a Methodist preacher, and it was a joyous day, made even gladder by the growing family God had given the Buntains. During the first few happy years, God blessed the Buntains with a beautiful baby boy and later a charming girl. Alec and Alice were the pride of their preacher parents. After ordination, Dan and Kathleen were assigned to a Methodist church in Winnipeg.

But the happy Buntain household was shattered when tragedy struck. It all started when they received word that Kathleen's sister back in Belleville had died suddenly. Dan could not leave his flock, but Kathleen took their two children to attend the funeral. As Kathleen and the two small children rode toward Belleville young Alec and Alice both became violently ill. Their frantic mother took her babies off the train and found a rooming house. Before help came, Alec died. The doctor said it was diphtheria.

Kathleen, alone, with one child dead and another

near death, desperately prayed that God would help her. She pleaded that God would spare her daughter and give her strength in the loss of her son.

She called Dan, and he rushed to join his wife in the town where their son had died. When their daughter was able to travel, they sadly took the dead boy's body on to Belleville, where he was buried in the same grave as Kathleen's sister. But God had spared little Alice Buntain and as the days passed she grew stronger.

Another child was born into the Buntain household and it was a second little boy. The grief over their loss began to dissipate, but then this new baby boy became ill. Mastoiditis killed him in a matter of days.

The parents were crushed, but their faith remained firm: like a nail, the harder it was hit, the deeper it went into the wood. Dan and Kathleen began to pray fervently that God would give them another son. They promised, like Hannah of old, that if God would answer their prayers, the boy would be given to preach the gospel.

Within a few months Kathleen began to feel a familiar stirring in her body. She knew instinctively that a faithful God had answered her prayers. She also knew what she would name the child. This boy would be an evangelist who would tell the lost about the Lord they loved. His name should be "Mark," and like his namesake he would be set aside to tell the blessed gospel of Jesus and His power to heal and save.

Mark was two years old when God blessed the Dan Buntains with still another son. Little Fulton would also grow up to be a great preacher, pastoring one of the largest churches in North America, and a great enthusiast and sponsor of his older brother's ministry.

Meanwhile, Mark's father had gained the love and respect of the citizens of Winnipeg. He was pastoring a prospering Methodist congregation and well on the rise to leadership in the Methodist conference. But then, the destiny of the Buntain family was dramatically altered.

The change came in the person of a fiery pentecostal preacher named Dr. Charles Price. Already well known throughout the United States, Price invaded Canada with a "strange new message."

Dan Buntain was furious that such false doctrine was fanning like a wind-whipped prairie fire over his country. When Price came to Winnipeg, the Methodist cleric determined to run him out of the city. Dan stormed the city officials' offices demanding that they refuse to rent Price an auditorium. When this failed, Dan publicly warned his people and the press to have nothing to do with the pentecostal preacher.

But Price succeeded in obtaining the Winnipeg arena in spite of Buntain's opposition. And Buntain's own congregation began to be affected.

Dan had five young ladies in his church who were somewhat on the wild side. They attended church, but they were also known to frequently imbibe things of the world. It bothered Dan that they were not dedicated. Although they were not morally evil, they were careless about spiritual things. They all worked at the local brewery.

One Wednesday evening during the regular Methodist Bible study and prayer meeting, these five girls showed up in Dan Buntain's church. After the study, the pastor called the people to prayer, and to his amazement these five girls came and began to pray fervently.

Before long, tears washed down their faces, and then they suddenly began praying in a language Buntain had never heard before. He knew they had not learned it. He knew by the expressions on their faces that something had happened to them. He also saw their dramatically altered life style during the next few days, and he knew that what had happened to them was genuine.

Then Dan learned they had been to one of Price's pentecostal meetings and had "gone forward." So he decided it was time to take a first-hand look at what was going on down at the arena.

"Can you get me a seat where I can see everyone, but they can't see me?" Buntain asked an usher at the meeting. "I've got just the seat for you," the man replied. He took Dan Buntain up a long catwalk to a room hanging from the ceiling where the orchestra sat when it played for the arena's ice skating shows. When Dan opened the door he found a Baptist preacher already inside—he had also come to see what was happening.

Later the usher came back to sell Dr. Price's hymn books.

"We had better investigate this doctrine before we buy their literature," the Baptist preacher said.

But Dan Buntain bought a hymn book anyway, and hesitantly sang with the happy congregation that night.

After Price had preached a stirring sermon, he called sinners to come forward. He then prayed for the sick. "For the first time," Dan said later, "I saw the power of Pentecost. People were healed. I was the last person out of the building. I saw the janitors lock the door."

Something strange had happened to Mark Buntain's dad that night. Rather than taking a streetcar, he walked the five miles home, praying all the way. At times he had his hands raised toward heaven, crying out to God. "I was just hungry for God," he recalled in later years. "As I walked I just said, 'Lord, am I wrong, am I wrong? Is this pentecostal message real?'"

Pastor Buntain was so troubled by what he saw that he announced to his congregation he was taking a month's leave of absence to try to sort things out. Dan went to a log cabin he had built for relaxation on the shores of Lake Winnipeg. There he prayed, fasted and studied God's Word for hours. He was determined to know what God said about this new experience.

When Pastor Buntain came back to Winnipeg, he announced he would preach a series of messages on "Why I Do Not Believe in Pentecostal Baptism."

The next Sunday he started the series with great anticipation. But, before long, he preached himself under conviction. In the middle of one of the sermons, Dan began to cry uncontrollably. He ran from his pulpit to the vestry and threw himself on his knees by the desk. Startled deacons came running into the office.

"What's wrong?" they asked. "Brethren, I'll never preach another sermon," Pastor Buntain replied, "until God baptizes me with the Holy Ghost." Although, of course, it was impossible for him to keep this pledge, it did emphasize how deeply Dan desired God's move.

News like this travels fast. It wasn't long before leaders of the Methodist Conference heard that Dan Buntain had endorsed Pentecost. According to the prevailing rumors, he had not personally had the "second blessing," but he was embracing this dangerous doctrine.

At the next conference, Buntain was told he would have to leave the Methodist church if he did not recant. But he could not take such a stand. He had seen too much, and he knew it was of God.

The same afternoon, the Methodist superintendent stood in the conference session and announced, "The first order of business today is that the Reverend Daniel Newton Buntain has endorsed the pentecostal message. We declare he is no longer a part of this conference. Would he please stand up and leave the floor."

To make matters worse, Kathleen was pregnant again. How would a defrocked clergyman feed his pregnant wife and two small children?

The Holy Spirit had fallen in a remarkable way on the city of Winnipeg following Dr. Price's meetings. There was a group of pentecostal believers who had been asked to leave their former churches and did not have a pastor for their newly formed congregation. The group heard that Dan had been thrown out of his church, and they sent for him.

"Would you come and be our pastor?" they asked. He replied honestly, "I can't come. I'm not filled with the Spirit myself."

But the little group knew this move was of God.

"You come," they said, "and we will pray that God will fill you with the Spirit." Mark's dad accepted the pastorate of that little church and later it became one of the most influential pentecostal churches in Canada.

Mark says of those days, "I remember looking up into my dad's face while he was preaching and saying, 'I want to be a preacher.' "

Dan Buntain was desperately hungry to be filled with the Holy Spirit. He sought God and searched through the Word. He was seeing others filled with the Spirit, but nothing was happening to him. Even Kathleen, now a new mother again, had received the baptism. Dan was wondering if God would ever answer his deep yearning to be filled.

One night in the church's prayer room, the power of God began to fall in a wonderful way. One man in the congregation, a manager of the toy department in a leading department store, experienced the pentecostal blessing.

When Dan saw the glory break in this man's life, he thought he could no longer bear his hunger. The preacher got down on his knees and begged the Lord to fill him.

In the midst of that prayer, Dan suddenly remembered an incident that had occurred some years before. Dan had worked in the Goose Lake River country of Saskatchewan. During that time he had traveled often on the train, but, because he knew the conductor, he rarely paid the fare.

In this moment of prayer, Dan knew that what he had done was wrong. He got up quickly from his knees and went into the office. He sat down and wrote a short note to Canadian Pacific Railway, telling them what he had done. He wrote out a check for the total amount of his stolen fares and put the check in an envelope. He gave it to his secretary for the next morning's mail.

Now his heart was clean; he was right with God. Dan went back into the prayer room and just as he got down on his knees, the power of God struck his life and God filled him with the Holy Spirit, manifested through a glorious unknown language.

In that beautiful moment, the former Methodist preacher had a glorious vision of the Lord Jesus Christ. That vision was so real that many years later he often stopped preaching in the middle of the sermon to tell how he came face to face with the Lord Jesus Christ. It was to be his greatest spiritual experience.

5

Eating the Orange

The Buntains were people of great faith even in small things. "My parents trusted God," Mark remembers. "We had a little bulldog we loved much. One summer we went to our log cabin on Lake Winnipeg to spend a month. Our little bulldog, Trixie, was unusual.

"She never paid much attention to the car and never came around it at all. But when the month of July came along, somehow she knew it was vacation time. Then she would not leave our car. She would hang around, sitting by the wheels, waiting for us to leave for the beach and enjoy our holiday.

"That summer we were about to leave the house for vacation. Our dog had eaten some bad food somewhere and, as we were driving along in that old

Ford, Trixie became violently ill. We thought she was dying.

"We were driving along the sandy trails by Winnipeg Beach, and dad stopped the car. He dug a hole in the sand to find a cool place for our puppy. We children were crying and upset.

"When we prayed in the family we always got in a circle. So we all got down on our knees around the little dog. We laid our hands on little Trixie, and our father in that marvelous faithful prayer asked Jesus to heal the dog.

"In that moment Trixie jumped up out of the hole, leaped back up into the car, and was ready to continue our trip. These were the impressions that were left on my young mind of how good God is and how well He answers prayer."

Another experience with Trixie reinforced the concept of God's care for all His creatures in Mark's life. "Up in that northern country," he recalls, "we lost our dog. We couldn't find her anywhere. It was very heavily forested country. We searched all around, but still no Trixie. There was one place about a half-mile from our cottage which we called the 'lonesome pine' because one tree stood taller than the other. Once again dad called us together, and we got down on our knees in a circle to pray. We asked Jesus to help us find our little bulldog.

"After prayer, we got into our Ford and drove down the sandy trail. Why my father was led to go in that direction, and not in the other, only God could tell. We stopped near the lonesome pine. Dad opened the door, and called, 'Trixie.' She came and jumped up into the automobile. These are the simple things in my early young life that let me know Jesus is real."

Mark's conversion to Christ was deep and moving. When he talks about it, he still weeps.

"I will never forget one Sunday afternoon," Mark says, "when a dear lady was speaking to our open session of Sunday school. My teacher, Christine Matheson, stood next to me, and when the lady gave an altar call, asking the boys and girls to give their lives to Christ, my Sunday school teacher leaned down and said, 'Mark, if you will go forward and give your life to Jesus, I will go with you.' She came with me up the aisle and knelt with me that day. In that old church, I gave my heart to Jesus.

"I remember going home and I was a changed boy. I knew I had been changed. My younger brother, Fulton, was always quite a tease, and he loved to upset me. My only defense was to try to hit him, and when I got home from Sunday school, my brother came in from the back door. He was in one of his teasing moods, and I remember instantly saying to myself, 'I gave my heart to Jesus today; I can't strike him back.' I recall so well that I had a change of heart, and I thank God with all my soul that from that time Jesus has never left me. Through all of my school years, Jesus was always my very, very dear friend."

Mark was thirteen when a mighty revival swept through Winnipeg.

Two young evangelists from North Dakota had walked into his father's church study one morning and said boldly, "We are evangelists and we want to conduct a meeting in this city. Could we use your church?"

The Spirit of God spoke to Dan Buntain, and he replied, "We will begin Sunday."

For fifteen weeks the glory of God settled on the city. Although it was bitterly cold with heavy snows, each Sunday the church was forced to have multiple services. One crowd waited out in the cold for the other crowd to finish.

During this time Mark experienced his personal infilling of the Holy Spirit.

Although his friends were being filled with the Spirit, young Mark somehow could not seem to touch God. He was having the same struggle his dad had experienced. He began wondering why God was delaying.

Mark knew that when his parents wanted something desperately from God, they often fasted. He did not know much about fasting, but he did know it meant you didn't eat. He decided to try it.

Saturday came, and Mark wanted the baptism of the Holy Spirit so badly he determined not to eat until he was filled. That day, he had to go across the city on the streetcar for his piano lesson. He had managed to get by without eating any breakfast and was able to succeed in not eating any lunch. But by now, Mark was terribly hungry. Tempted, he slipped an orange in his pocket and went on to his piano lesson.

Mark remembers walking back through the Lord Robert's school ground when he became so hungry he could hardly bear it. Still, he wanted Jesus to fill him with the Holy Spirit in the Sunday service. While the spirit is willing, the flesh is often weak and Mark's hunger got the best of him. He ate the orange, and he still recalls the moment.

"Standing there in the schoolyard I thought, 'Oh, my, now Jesus won't fill me with the Holy Spirit tomorrow.' I got home, and to my dismay my parents had invited company for supper. Of course, that would mean it was going to be difficult to get by without eating the evening meal. My father called me for supper, and I went and sat down and ate with the family. I thought within my heart, 'Oh, my, now Jesus certainly won't fill me with the Holy Spirit tomorrow.' "

Sunday came and the great meeting was on. The power of God surged through the church. That morning Mark saw a totally blind youth instantly healed. The blind boy became so excited he ran around the church several times. There were other dramatic miracles.

But even though it was a great service, Mark was still not filled.

That Sunday night Mark played his trumpet in the

church orchestra. The area for the orchestra platform was raised, so the audience could see the orchestra. Mark sat on the front row.

When the evangelist finished preaching he said, "I believe the first person to the prayer room tonight will be filled with the Holy Spirit."

Mark dropped his horn on the floor with a clatter. He ran to the prayer room amid the people's laughter, but he didn't care. Like those at the Pool of Bethesda, he wanted to be there first. In the prayer room, Mark raised his hand and began crying out to God to fill him with the Holy Spirit.

"I became as light as a feather," Mark says, recalling that experience, "and I simply floated back until I was lying on the floor. I had a slingshot in my pocket. We lived on the edge of the city in a rural community with heavy trees, next to the main railroad lines. We boys often used our slingshots to knock insulators off the telephone poles. We liked to see those porcelain insulators split. One afternoon while we were shooting insulators, a man came up the tracks wearing a long brown overcoat and felt hat. He stopped us and showed us his badge. To our dismay he was a railway policeman. He took our names and addresses, wrote them in his book, and went away.

"Lying there on the floor praying, I remembered that if I had anything wrong in my life, Jesus would not fill me with the Holy Spirit. I didn't know what to do. The slingshot was in my hip pocket. But I was hungry for God, so I reached into my back pocket, took out my slingshot, and tried to hide it under the small of my back. I didn't know people were around me, because I was lost in prayer. I was trying to get all of the sin out of my life and foolishly tried to hide my slingshot from God. I wanted my heart to be right with God.

"Kneeling beside me was Dan Campbell, a detective on the Winnipeg city police force. Brother Dan saw that slingshot when I reached for it. He knew what was troubling me. He reached under, covered the weapon with his big hand and slipped it into his own coat pocket.

"At that moment God chose to fill me with His Holy Spirit. I praised God until about one o'clock in the morning. That was the beginning of His great blessing in my life."

Not long after the Winnipeg revival, another dramatic change came to young Mark's life. His father was asked to become superintendent of the new Pentecostal Assemblies of Canada. This meant a move from Winnipeg to the bustling city of Toronto. Although Mark had some reservations about leaving Winnipeg where he had so many friends, still his thirteen-year-old heart did look forward to the new excitement of a great city.

Mark found the school system of Toronto more difficult, and he had a hard time adjusting. He attended Danforth Technical School with more than 3,000 teen-agers. As far as he could tell, he was the only born-again believer in the entire school.

The elder Buntains were always strict with their children and demanded they earn their own way as soon as they were able to work. In those days the lot of a preacher was always a poor one, so even as the prestigious head of a religious denomination, Dan Buntain earned barely enough to keep his little family going.

Each of the Buntain children had housework to do. Each Saturday morning, Mother Buntain took a piece of paper and wrote each child's name and work assignments on it. Saturday was a day when other children played football and hockey, but the Buntains couldn't enjoy any of these sports until chores were finished.

Mark's job was to wash the basement floor. His mother taught him to cook and bake. Little did he know that one day he would teach those same practical lessons to Indians in the busy kitchens of his Calcutta ministry.

When Mark turned sixteen, his mother talked to the general manager of Don Avon Market, one of Toronto's largest chain stores, and asked if her son could have a job. He got the job, and he was proud to be employed and earning money on his own. Mark hurried home from school on Fridays, running several blocks, quickly changed his clothes, and caught a streetcar to work. He worked until 11 P.M. on Friday and all day Saturday.

Mark had only been at the store a few weeks when

on Saturday night he was left alone. The manager had told him to stay.

As he waited at the cash register, he noticed a dollar bill lying on the floor. The tempter's voice told Mark to pick it up and put it in his pocket, since his pay for working twenty-five hours was only $1.25.

But, the years of training and Mark's love for his Master prevailed. He took that dollar back through the store until he found the grocery manager. "Sir," Mark said, "I found this dollar on the floor at the cash register."

The manager thanked Mark and sent him home. Next Saturday the store filled with customers. Mark sacked groceries at the cash register. He was working hard when the general manager of the entire chain of stores came and took him away from the check-out area. He took Mark to the back of the store and handed him a brown wicker basket full of paper bags. The bags were obviously stuffed to capacity. The manager told Mark to watch the basket and not to leave it.

Mark stood there from 4:00 P.M. until 10:00 that night.

Finally the manager came back and asked, "Do you know what was in those bags?"

Mark replied that he had not looked in them.

"Well," the manager said, "those bags contain $4,000." Then he told Mark he had put the dollar bill on the floor to test him. As an additional test, he had made him stand by the sack of money.

And before Mark turned eighteen, he was named a department manager of one of Toronto's largest stores.

During this time Mark faced his first real test from God. He loved music, and played his trumpet at church each week. He also played in the high school orchestra. Mark was good enough that several other school orchestra members wanted him involved with them, playing for weekend dances. They offered Mark more money than he was making as a manager.

Mark turned them down. He loved the Lord and didn't want to do anything wrong.

"But, you know," Mark says, "there was a part of my heart I had not yet yielded to the Lord. God knew that place was there and it had to be dealt with."

God dealt with Mark through an accident. One Saturday afternoon, while he was working in the store's shipping department, Mark picked up a wooden case of canned food, and threw it across the floor to the delivery truck. When he did, a sliver of wood jammed into the palm of his hand. Mark didn't pay any attention to the injury and went on with his work.

The next morning, while he was at church, Mark felt a sharp pain in the palm of his hand. He looked down and saw that the sliver had begun to fester. He flicked the sore with his thumb and pushed the splinter out. But, during the day, he noticed his hand becoming hot and swollen.

That Sunday night, he slept only fitfully. He awoke in the morning with a deep red line from his wrist, all along his arm. It was obvious he had blood poisoning.

Through the day, Mark's fever shot up—and the dark red line deepened. The family finally called a doctor. The old, white-haired physician told Mark he had a streptococcus infection. This was serious, since Terramycin had not been developed and the illness could be life-threatening. In an effort to draw out the poison, the doctor applied an old-fashioned hot poultice.

Five days passed, and Mark's fever raged. His hand was wrapped in a linseed poultice with a heating pad around it. The doctor hoped the heat of the poultice would help to stay the infection.

During the illness, Mark had not slept well. Now exhaustion took over and he drifted off to sleep. The hot pad cooked the linseed oil into Mark's flesh. When he awoke his hand was horribly baked and he had lost all feeling in the limb.

After a few days, Mark was desperately ill. One afternoon at his lowest point, a local pastor's wife came and stood at the edge of Mark's doorway. "Mark, I've come to pray for you," she said. In that moment, God spoke to Mark's heart, and asked for a complete surrender of his life. "In the time it took her to step from my doorway over to my bed," Mark recalls, "I said yes to Jesus."

Mrs. Swanson laid one hand on Mark's head and her other hand on his arm. As she prayed, Mark was instantly healed. They both saw the red line disappear from Mark's arm, and Mark could feel the fever leave his body.

The old country doctor shopped at the market where Mark worked. After that day, every time he came into the store, he took Mark's hand and said, "This is a miracle, this is a miracle."

But the greatest test of all was still ahead.

6

Gone the Glory

Although Mark's commitment was sure, he still would be challenged again concerning how he was going to spend his life. This time the battleground would not be his physical health. This battle raged in his ambitions and desires.

As he approached manhood, Mark's desire to be a preacher decreased. The thought of becoming a musician or a radio announcer became more and more appealing. These ambitions began to crowd in on Mark, upsetting his spiritual equilibrium.

Radio, still in its "golden days," was fascinating to many of the young men of Mark's day. For years he had followed the wonders of this medium. His earliest encounter with the broadcasting world came when Mark's father came home to announce he had purchased time on a local radio station for their church choir to sing.

Mark remembers being terribly excited and insisting on going with his dad to see the broadcast. Mark was small, and his dad hesitated. But the boy's tears prevailed, and Dan Buntain let him go along, even though young Mark had to stay out in the hall and watch through a studio window.

"Bob Staggard introduced the choirs," Mark recalls with a glint in his eye, still remembering the announcer's name after all these years. "Oh, it was a glorious moment. I watched with my tiny nose pressed flat against the glass and my little heart pounding hard. I had never seen anything so exciting. From that moment on I said, 'One day I am going to be a radio announcer.' "

Mark's fascination with radio continued as the years spun by. He often sat up late at night with his ears glued to a small radio receiver, listening for station calls far away. He could identify every announcer in all the cities his set could receive.

One summer the Buntains decided they would drive their family car all the way from Winnipeg to Boston to visit Mark's aunt and uncle. It was an unheard of thing to do during those days when highways were little more than dirt roads. People said it was terrible to take children so far in a car. They predicted the Buntains would never return.

Yet Mark and his family made the trip and arrived safely in Boston. They had an exciting time, and on the last Saturday of their visit, their hosts had arranged a picnic down by the sea. The family was scheduled to go to the beach for the picnic at noon, but Mark pleaded with his aunt to wait until after 1:30 in the afternoon. She quietly agreed, not knowing why Mark was so insistent. But Mark wanted to wait in Boston because at 1:30 radio station WHWH, the fisherman's station, came on with the world news and weather report. Mark wanted to hear their announcer more than he wanted a day at the beach. He began to live for the day he would stand in front of the microphone and become a famous radio personality.

That dream almost came true. His managerial job led directly into the world of radio. The man who had hired Mark at the store was a board member of the famed Casa Loma, the only genuine castle built on the North American continent. It had been built by Sir Henry Pellett as a Canadian home for Queen Victoria. The fabulous ninety-eight-room structure attracts thousands of tourists annually and employs scores of tour guides. Although she never personally visited the castle or its beautiful garden, the palace did house the queen's rifle regiment at one time.

The old castle had become a public park, operated by the local Kiwanis Club. Mark's manager recommended him as a tour guide so Mark started his new and important job, feeling that things were looking bright for his future. All the other guides were college students, and Mark was thrust into a new intellectual environment. On Saturday nights, the castle was turned into a ballroom for dances. He began to see and hear things that were foreign to his sheltered life.

Although Mark didn't receive a salary for his tour guide work, he did receive tips from patrons and tourists and he made a lot of money. In fact, he made much more money than was good for him.

Mark also discovered an additional source of income. He noticed it took one hour and fifteen minutes to complete each tour. He began to see some tourists who visited the palace but did not have time for a full tour. They were always disappointed, so Mark quietly slipped alongside them and offered a unique service on his own.

"I see you can't stay for the full time," he said, "but I will be happy to show you what I can."

He would quickly show them an abbreviated version of the tour and collect a fat tip for his special effort.

Soon Mark was hungering for money.

"I was doing anything I could to make money," he recalls, "and I was making plenty of it. But God was continuing to speak to my heart. I remember the strength of His conviction was still in my life. During my off-hours at the castle, I still went out onto the big marble piazzas and sat with my Bible, letting God speak to my heart."

One dark Sunday Mark will never forget. For the first time he had been asked to work on the Lord's day. At 9:00 A.M. Mark called a taxi to take him to the castle.

Dad Buntain met him at the door. "Where are you going?" he asked.

"Going to work," Mark replied.

"No one in this house works on Sunday," Mark's dad said. "You know that."

"Dad, I'm sorry," Mark replied. "I can't live by that rule, I have to go."

He stepped out into the street and went off to work. He was eighteen years old and had taken the first tiny step toward rebellion.

Mark still weeps, nearly forty years later, when he recalls this incident.

"That Sunday was one of the most miserable days of my life. I didn't enjoy a minute of my work. I couldn't wait until the day was through. After work, I got onto the streetcar and went down to my home church. The service was over, and only the caretaker was there.

"I went upstairs to the prayer room and got down on my knees. I begged God, for Jesus' sake, to please forgive me. I knew I was not in His will. I knew I was not doing what God wanted me to do."

Two things pulled at Mark during that time. First was his desire to serve God, and next was his desire for a radio career. Because of Mark's contact with the Kiwanis Club and the castle, he soon was asked to be a broadcaster with radio station CFCO in Chatham, Ontario. It was Canada's first and most popular radio station.

He loved his work. His childhood dreams were coming true. On many nights, he actually took the other announcer's shifts just so he could be on the air.

When he took the radio job, Mark left home and moved to Chatham. There he boarded with a pentecostal pastor and his wife, the Sammy Wilsons. Mrs. Wilson had been one of the five girls who had worked in the brewery years before and had been saved in Dr. Price's Winnipeg meetings.

Things went well for the preacher's son on the radio. He became the station's leading jazz disc jockey. He enjoyed broadcasting news of the Russian-Finnish War and being a stand-by announcer for commercials during the exciting Joe Louis prize fights. His jazz music show brought the station its highest ratings.

Still, something nagged deep within the heart of Mark Buntain.

"There is one Saturday night," Mark says, "I'll never forget as long as I live. I left the boarding home to do my night work. I stepped into the elevator in the beautiful William Pitt Hotel, where our studios were located, and shot up to the fourth floor. As I stepped out of the elevator, something happened to me. I felt the glory of God leave my life.

"It frightened me. I went down to my studio and tried to do my work. That evening, Pastor Wilson had brought a friend who wanted to see a radio broadcast in progress. They were sitting in the studio. Perspiration began to run down my face and over my shirt. They asked, 'Why are you perspiring so tonight?' I didn't answer them. God was dealing with my heart.

"Before long Pastor Wilson and his friend left the studio. I went on with my midnight news from the British Press. Later I turned off the switch, said good night to the engineer, and headed home. I remember walking through a schoolyard; the sky was so bright. The stars were shining, and I knew God was pleading with my life.

"When I got home, dear Mrs. Wilson had my midnight supper waiting for me. I sat down, but I couldn't eat. Tears began to run down my face. She asked, 'What's wrong?' I said, 'Sister Wilson, I have to get out of radio.' She raised her hands and cried. 'Thank God, this is what we have been praying for.' I didn't know anyone was praying for me except my parents back home in Toronto.

"I went into my bedroom," Mark continues, "and about one-thirty in the morning I got down on my knees by my bed. I lifted up my hands and cried, 'God, if you can take the craving for this world out of my heart, this desire for jazz and this desire for money, I promise you I will preach the gospel.' "

The change was obvious to Mark's employers and it promptly ruined his radio career.

"The next morning I went to my studio," he remembers, "but the old false Mark was gone. That false voice you learn to generate for radio had left me. I was just simple and plain."

Mark's production manager, Pete Kirky, came running into the studio.

"Mark, you are no good!" he yelled. Mark didn't even bother to answer him; he knew he was no good.

The next morning the station manager called Mark into his office.

"What's wrong?" he asked.

"I want to leave radio."

"But you can't go! You're under contract to us."

"Please," Mark begged, "I want to leave."

"Why do you want to go?"

"I want to preach the gospel of Jesus Christ."

The manager paused. "If that's your reason," he sighed, "you can go. But you have to wait until we can get someone to take your place."

Once the commitment was made, Mark could hardly wait to get out. The radio station advertised in the *Toronto Star*. Soon a young man was hired and Mark was released.

Mark says, "I remember how with utmost joy I ran down four flights of stairs, out of that hotel, and into the street. I was free to serve the Lord, and I praised Him with all my heart."

Mark was still boarding with the Wilsons, and now that he had no job, he didn't know what to do. But in the next few weeks, he was driven to his knees. From that first night when he knelt by his bed, he had an insatiable desire and burden for prayer. "I didn't want to do anything but pray," Mark says. "I wanted to stay in my room and pray. I would pray during the day. I got up from my sleep to pray. People were beginning to think I was losing my mind.

"It was summertime, and others were going on picnics. But I didn't want to leave the house. I wanted to be left alone in my room to read God's Word and pray. I wanted to just be left alone with God."

The Wilsons became worried. Perhaps young Mark had gone off the deep end. They sent word to a pastor friend in Detroit. Dr. Klein was a prince of preachers and the pastor of a great church in that city. He would know what to do.

When Dr. Klein arrived, Mark was in his room praying. Mark glanced out the bedroom window which overlooked the front yard, and saw the preacher approaching. Silently, the Holy Spirit spoke to Mark: "This man has come to talk to you."

During the noon meal, Mark knew Dr. Klein was going to speak to him. Mark said nothing, but after lunch, Mark purposely walked to his bedroom. The pastor followed.

When the great preacher entered Mark's room, he asked, "What is happening to you? What is taking place in your life?"

Mark spilled out his experience—how God had been dealing with him at the radio studio, how he didn't want to do anything else but pray and read his

Bible.

When Mark finished, the pastor said, "When will you come and preach in my church?"

Mark was shocked, but the answer just fell out of his heart.

"I'll come in two weeks," Mark heard himself say.

Within a few days Mark left the Wilsons to return to his parents in Toronto. World War II had just started, and it was difficult to cross the border from Canada into the American city of Detroit. Mark didn't know how he would be able to keep his Detroit appointment. But Mark's dad, thrilled that his son's heart was turning toward the ministry, used all his resources to help Mark get his permit to cross the border so he could preach for Dr. Klein. He bade his son good-bye and sent him off to Detroit. Dan smiled as the train left. He had known all along that God would bring Mark around.

From the start, the Detroit revival was dramatic. God poured out His Spirit and blessed abundantly. Many were saved and touched by the love of the Lord. Mark knew he had made the right decision.

But Mark's lack of formal Bible training brought him a great moment of embarrassment. One day before he left the Wilsons in Chatham, Mark was reading the book of Zechariah. He read a story in which Satan was standing at Joshua's right hand to resist him.

Mark was fascinated by this story and asked Mrs.

Wilson, "Who is Joshua?"

She, busy in her kitchen, replied quickly, "You know Joshua; he was with Moses."

Mark accepted that answer, and began to think that this would make a wonderful sermon.

So, several Sunday afternoons later, in the huge church in Detroit, with its balcony packed and hundreds of people in the audience, Mark preached on Joshua, who had been with Moses.

He told how Satan had stood at his right hand to resist him.

It was a moving sermon, so powerful that an old deacon ran up on the platform, swung his arms out to the crowd, and called for souls to come to the altar.

The effect was staggering. Scores came streaming down those aisles to fall at the mourner's bench.

Dr. Klein said nothing to Mark about the message. But, some time later Mark was in Alberta preaching for another outstanding minister. He remembered the Detroit meeting and decided to preach on Joshua again. Mark pulled out the same sermon outline he had used in Dr. Klein's church and again preached with enthusiasm and zeal.

It was a good sermon and had the desired effect. But on the way home, the pastor said kindly, "Mark, if I were you I would get my Joshuas straight."

"I'll never forget how stunned I was," Mark says. "Then I began to realize there were two Joshuas in the Old Testament.

"Well, I felt so bad I didn't know what to do. But

the Lord helped me, and I realized that if I got up on Sunday morning and preached on the right Joshua, I would get it straightened out. This way the devil didn't have the advantage over me any more."

It was a bitter pill to swallow, but Mark made things right.

By now the war was heating to such intensity that Canada was drafting its own young men as soldiers. Some of Mark's friends had already been killed overseas. Others from the church in Toronto had come back medically discharged, suffering horribly from the wounds of war. About two weeks before his birthday Mark had received a card in the mail saying he would soon be drafted. But a friend told Mark that if they would enlist before they received the final card, they could choose which branch of service they wanted. If they waited, they had to enlist in the infantry. Mark and his friend decided to enlist.

Then walking down Queen Street in Toronto, the boys saw a sign: "Enlist today in the Royal Canadian Mounted Police."

That was the answer!

"Let's go," Mark said.

They walked in and both enlisted.

His friend was three months older than Mark, so the recruiter told the other boy, "We'll take you first." He told Mark not to leave the Toronto area without their permission, and that he would be sent with a second group of boys to the Royal Canadian Mounted Police boot camp in Ottawa. There was little he could do but go home and wait.

Still, Mark continued praying and seeking God. "I loved the Lord with all my heart," he recalls, "and I did have some beautiful experiences in prayer. But God knew there was something much deeper that still had to be done in my life."

Mark's mother also knew she had not raised Mark to be a soldier, but a preacher. So one Sunday, while he was waiting for his draft notice, she said to Mark, "Why don't you drive down with us to the camp meeting at Braeside?"

Conflict raged inside Mark's heart as he drove the family car to the camp meeting. He did not know what to do. God had called him to preach, but he also had a commitment to his country.

When he arrived that Sunday evening, thousands were already overrunning the famed campsite. Mark didn't go inside the meeting.

"A battle was on in my life again," he says, "for that complete surrender. I stood outside and watched from the outside of the big open tabernacle. Finally the speaker, the Reverend Aaron Wilson, preached. The power of God was on that dear, great man, and hundreds were praying. I walked around in back of the tabernacle and was standing on the left side, watching many people pray and kneel in the sawdust. The power of God was heavy in that place.

"An army chaplain walked up behind me and laid his hand on my shoulder. He said, 'Mark, why don't you praise the Lord with these people?' I really thought I should do more confessing than praising, but I knew there was still something God was trying to do in my life, even though I didn't understand what it was. But I did want to obey God.

"I lifted my hand and began to ask the Lord to help me. The moment I did, my feet began to move under me, and I thought, 'Oh, no.' Some time before I had said to my mother, 'There is one thing I will never do and that is dance in the Spirit.'

"As I stood there with my hands raised I felt the anointing of the Spirit begin to flow through my life. My feet began to move. I felt they were moving in a perfect pattern under me. I tried to stop them. I dug them deep into the sawdust, but the more I tried to stop them, it seemed the faster they moved. I knew it was God, because my feet were forming a perfect pattern I could never do myself.

"I knew something more, and that was I didn't dare resist the Holy Spirit. That was one thing my parents had taught me most fervently. They drilled into my head that we must never grieve the Holy Spirit.

"In my heart I said, 'Yes, Lord, whatever you want for me is what I want.' In that moment I had the only vision I've ever experienced. Instantly, I was completely lost to my surroundings, and in front of me I saw waves and waves of Chinese people, and I was preaching to them. The harder I preached, the faster they came to Jesus, wave upon wave. This experience began about 9:00 in the evening. When I opened my eyes it was about 1:00 in the morning.

"All the people from the tabernacle had retired to their tents and cottages. It was raining and the sky was black outside. I was all alone. When I opened my eyes I knew God had called me to preach the gospel and one day I would be a missionary. I was sure it would be to China.

"I jumped up and ran over to my mother's cottage where she was in bed. She had not been well those days, and I picked her right up off the pillow. I put my arms under her and lifted her up saying through my tears, 'Oh, mother, Jesus has called me to preach.' She said, 'Yes, Mark, I know He has. You had better get to bed.' "

After the camp experience Mark went back to Toronto to await his call to the armed services. Before it came, the Saskatchewan Conference of the Pentecostal Assemblies of Canada met in Saskatoon. During that conclave, the executives told Mark's dad they had a small town where their church had no pastor. They could not afford to hire an established preacher and they didn't know what to do.

"We have no young men," they told Dan Buntain. "They have all been called up into the service. Do you know anyone who could help us?"

"There is only one boy I know of," Mark's dad replied, "who may be able to help us. He's had a little preaching experience. That's my own son."

The conference officially wrote to the Royal Canadian Mounted Police and asked if Mark could be deferred, because they needed him in Watrous, Saskatchewan. They agreed.

"I remember my father calling me," Mark says. "I was down at Cardinal, Ontario, in a youth meeting. Dad announced through the phone, 'Mark, we want you to go and pastor a church in Watrous, Saskatchewan.'

"I remember how bitterly I wept. I didn't want to go. Any young Canadian not going in the armed forces was a terrible disgrace to his country. I didn't want to be a slacker or a weakling. I wanted to stay with the RCMP, but my father told me I should be obedient."

Mark Buntain was being called to yield his complete will to God. It was a test of obedience—a step in preparing him for his strange destiny.

7

Let Me Out

Temperatures in Saskatchewan average from −23°F to +10°F in the long hard winters. It is a lonely land where wheat and barley fields stretch to the horizon in all directions.

Mark's new little hometown sat huddled in the middle of a vast prairie, halfway between Regina and Saskatoon. Barely more than a thousand people lived in the lonely prairie town, and Mark did not know one of them.

To make matters worse, he arrived in the middle of the night and was put up in the town's only hotel. It was a seedy rattrap run by an Indian witch doctor and his wife.

Mark slept little. He left the solitary naked light bulb burning all night to keep the rats and insects at bay.

It was not a good start for a nineteen-year-old beginner.

Mark's instructions were to go across town to the O.K. Economy Store, where the owner would give him a key to the church parsonage. Rumpled from loss of sleep and his worry about the night creatures, Mark made his way to the store. He had all his worldly possessions with him: a beat-up suitcase and a cardboard box of old sermon books his dad had given him. Mark trudged through the muddy streets, finding his way from stone to stone.

"You will live in the last house on the outside of town, down this road," the man told Mark.

The man was right. It was the *last* house on the very edge of town. Mark turned the skeleton key in the dilapidated door and stepped into the tiny cottage; dust choked the air as he closed the door.

The ladies of the church thought their preacher would have a wife, so they had put an ample supply of wild plums on his table as a welcoming gift in case she wanted to make jam. Mark did not have a wife, and at that moment he wished he didn't have a church either.

"I sat down and bawled," Mark says, remembering that lonely moment. "I sobbed because I was so far from home. I didn't want to be in this place."

Before long, however, he pulled himself together and decided he could not change the circumstances.

He had better just make the best of it.

Mark hung up his clothes and trudged back to the store to ask where the church was. This time the manager sent him in the opposite direction. He would find a small shop on the left side of the road that had been turned into a church.

He learned there were six people in the congregation, including children.

Mark tried his best. He wanted to please the Lord, but he longed for the day when he could leave this storefront ministry. He knew there was only one man who could get him out of this predicament, and that was his father, the general superintendent of the Pentecostal Assemblies of Canada. He knew that soon his dad would make his annual journey across the country, and Mark encouraged himself with that thought.

"I'll wait for the day when dad comes," Mark said to himself, "and he will take me out of here. He couldn't expect me to do anything for God in Watrous."

In the meantime, Mark worked steadily. He came closest to success on the day he coaxed and begged twenty-one people into his church. A new record!

Not only was Mark the preacher of this church—he was also the janitor. Every Saturday night he had to get the little shop-church clean and set for Sunday. A young boy who attended the services helped Mark. They walked a mile to a small electric plant to get cleaning water, since there was no water at the church. The boys lugged two buckets of hot water back and scrubbed the floors of the church every Saturday night. They cringed to see the farmers stomp mud off their boots on the clean floor each Sunday.

Mark was proud of the church, but he was desperately lonely. Sundays were especially difficult.

"I would hope each week that, come Sunday, someone would invite me for a meal," Mark remembers. "One week I went to the store and bought two pork chops and brought them back to put in my 'refrigerator,' which was just a hole in the ground with a lid on it.

"After the Sunday morning service, a lady invited me to go home with her for lunch, but I remembered my two pork chops. I said, 'No thank you, may I please come next Sunday?' I excused myself and hurried home with my mouth set for a feast.

"When I lifted the wooden lid off the hole, I found the field rats had eaten my pork chops. I had to settle for bread and jam for Sunday dinner. God was teaching me lessons and speaking to my heart, and I am thankful for it."

Still, Mark continued to long for the day his father would come and take him out of Watrous. Finally, after many months, the day arrived. Mark was early to meet the 8:00 A.M. train. He ran to embrace his father and took him to the little parsonage.

As they walked toward the house, Mark tried to

speak to his dad about leaving, but the elder Buntain ignored him. When they reached the cottage, his father asked where Mark slept. Mark showed him the bed, and Dad Buntain crawled in and went to sleep.

After some time, he got up and worked on correspondence, saying very little to his son. Then he lay down and rested again.

Finally he asked, "Where can we go for lunch?"

Mark knew the time for talking had come.

"There is a Chinese restaurant up by the railway station," Mark answered.

They walked to the station and ate sausage and eggs. Mark was still waiting for his dad to say something about a transfer, but he never did.

Finally the two went back to the cottage where Dad Buntain worked on more letters. He got back into bed and went to sleep again.

Later Mark's father awoke and said, "Let's go back to that Chinese place for supper."

The train was to leave that night and still nothing had been said about a transfer. Mark was getting nervous. The father and son returned to the railway station and ate their meals.

After supper, the two walked back on the same cinder sidewalk. When they got to the schoolyard, the elder Buntain stopped. He looked Mark straight in the eyes and said, "Now, Mark, I know how you feel. You have one of two things you can do tonight. I will give you the money, and you can get on the train and go back to Toronto. Or you can stay here, stick it out and see what you can do for God in this place."

"I'll never forget the big, thick lump that came in my throat," Mark recalls. "Tears poured down my face, but I said, 'I will stay.' I count it as the turning point of my life, and I will be grateful to God as long as I live that He gave me the courage that night to say I would stick it out. If I had gone back to Toronto, I would have gone into the service and God only knows what would have happened to my life."

When the pressure was on, each of the Buntain children seemed to stand fast in the same firm resolve that their father faithfully demonstrated. Alice, Mark's older sister, was no exception.

"Alice was almost like a mother to Fulton and me," Mark says, "because our parents were always so busy in church work."

Mom Buntain was also a schoolteacher. When the Pentecostal Assemblies started a Bible school, they naturally asked her to help. They couldn't pay her, but her love for the Lord made Kathléen volunteer year after year. This left the three Buntain children at home much of the time, and Alice assumed most of the responsibility of keeping two active boys in tow.

When Alice entered her teen years, her voice developed to a rich and beautiful soprano. The Buntain parents recognized this unusual talent, and sent her to study under some of Canada's most recognized music instructors at the University of Toronto. She also attended the Conservatory of

Music and seemed destined for a music career. Even while she was still very young, Alice was asked to perform in concert with one of Japan's leading contraltos. Mark remembers the night of this performance: "I can see her now. She was dressed so beautifully with a long, lovely pink gown over tiny slippers. I was so proud."

Mark apparently had reason to be proud, because the Toronto papers gave excellent reviews of her singing and predicted great things for Alice Buntain.

After graduation Alice worked at the Royal Bank of Canada. Here she had many opportunities to date up-and-coming young men. A beautiful young lady, she loved the social life.

Before long a young millionaire proposed to her. "We can move to any city in the United States you desire," he promised. "Just say *yes!* You can have anything you want if you just marry me."

But deep down in young Alice's heart was that familiar call God had placed on each of the Buntains. She resisted and tried to still the inner voice, but she could never seem to succeed.

She knew her parents wanted her to go to Bible college in the States, but young Alice still rebelled in her spirit.

"Why can't I have a singing career and just give money to missionaries?" she asked her folks in a moment of pouting.

Finally, to please her parents, Alice decided to go to Central Bible College in Springfield, Missouri, for one term. After that, she determined, she would do what she wanted to do.

From the start, Alice decided to hate CBC. For weeks she refused to unpack her trunk or to apply herself to studies.

At the small midwestern college, all students were required to work; Alice drew one of the dirtiest jobs of all—washing the floors. With each stroke of the scrub brush, she detested the place more. Her aching, overworked muscles did their part too, intensifying her determination to escape this parental jail as soon as possible.

During one of the morning chapel services, the Spirit of God began to move in an unusual way. Students started to weep and confess the faults in their lives. W.I. Evans, a revered and saintly man, led the service. This would not be the last time this great old professor of the faith would influence the Buntain family.

That morning there was something in Evans's manner, something in the students' brokenness, that started to stir a chord deep within the heart of Alice. Hearing the faults of the other confessing students, Alice was overwhelmed by her own rebellion. All their faults seemed so small compared to what she was doing to her parents, her Lord, and herself.

Finally Alice stood up and spoke.

"I have been listening to all your confessions," she said through tears. "These are nothing compared to mine. I am here against my will."

She began to sob.

"I need your prayers," she choked out.

The students prayed. Dr. Evans prayed. And that day, Alice totally surrendered her heart to God. In that beautiful moment the burden of her rebellion was gone, and her life was surrendered to the Lord whom she loved in the deep recesses of her heart.

For the next two years, Alice worked hard at college and did well. Then she met a young man from the western part of the United States who was a missionary student and very popular on campus.

Alice was sure Edward Southard would never notice her. And, for a long time, it seemed he did not.

When her second year of school was over, Alice returned to Toronto, unsure whether to go back for a third and final year of training. She had been offered an attractive position in an excellent Canadian firm, and she wrestled with the decision.

Just as she reached the brink of decision to take the job, Alice received a long-distance phone call from Edward Southard. He asked her to be his guest at an alumni banquet at the school. She agreed, and from that first date their love bloomed.

Before too many months, Ed and Alice married.

The Southards have been pastors for many years. They have worked hard and built several beautiful congregations. In recent years a devastating heart attack struck Ed down, limiting his ministry. Today, however, Ed and Alice travel as field representatives for Mark Buntain's ministry, telling people everywhere about Jesus and the work Mark is doing in India.

8

The Pastor's Daughter

The determination that Dan and Kathleen Buntain instilled in their children has proven to be a great blessing to each of them. When Mark determined to stay in Watrous, God began to move in his life. Before long he was transferred to a larger church. Here he lived with a Christian family whose daughter was a nurse. She was in training in the hospital and, as a trainee, had to live at the hospital. This made her room at the house vacant, and the church group rented that room for their young bachelor pastor.

Mark earned five dollars a month as pastor of the church. It wasn't much, but his needs were small. He settled into the home routine, and life was not as lonely.

Mark was only there a short while when he saw the town had a radio station. This immediately fascinated him, and he got a group of young people together to form a radio choir. With the knowledge and skills he had picked up from radio broadcasting, he started "The Old-Fashioned Church of the Prairie" radio broadcast. It became a popular feature on Sunday afternoons to thousands of people in Central Canada and the United States.

During this time of his life Mark felt his first stirrings of young love. He had become fascinated with the young student nurse, Ruth, whose vacant room he had occupied. She always looked immaculate, and when he saw her in the hospital he was charmed by her abilities and attitude. (Even then there was something about hospitals that appealed to the young preacher. He loved to be there and minister.)

The friendship grew between these two young people. Mark knew Ruth's mother had ambitions for her to be in God's work. But somewhere deep down inside Mark's heart, something told him it just wasn't right. It was a personal struggle for him, but he gave up the girl. He wanted only God's will.

After leaving the tiny church, Mark served as an evangelist. He was sent up the Alcan Highway to preach at service camps in Dawson Creek. While he was there, he received an invitation from Pastor Alex Monroe in Vancouver, British Columbia. Vancouver, still very much a western town, was bursting with excitement. Monroe's was a sizable church for a struggling young evangelist. Mark was flattered, and decided to preach the revival crusade.

When the pastor met Mark at the railway station, he gave Mark the option of staying with a Christian family or in a hotel.

"I will stay where it will cost you the least money," Mark told the pastor.

On their way to the host family's residence, Pastor Monroe said, "We are going to have lunch with my daughter this afternoon. Would you like to join us?"

Mark said he would be delighted, although he had never met Huldah Monroe.

After depositing Mark's clothing where he would be staying, the pastor took the young preacher to lunch. Pastor Monroe's daughter worked in the courthouse as a reporter. She also was head stenographer in the land registry office. As soon as they picked up Huldah, Mark was star struck. She was wearing a chocolate brown suit and a matching brown broad-brimmed hat. He didn't think he had ever seen a more beautiful girl.

Looking back now, Mark says, "I tried not to pay too much attention to anyone or anything at the time. My heart was really settled on the fact that this was the first night of our campaign and I wanted God's mightiest blessings for sure.

"But, as I stood up to speak that evening, I glanced down the center aisle, and this young lady, the pastor's daughter, was sitting halfway back in the audience. At that moment something in my heart said, 'You are going to marry that girl.' "

Still, Mark had made a covenant with the Lord on the train ride from the Alcan Highway to Vancouver. He told the Lord he wanted to leave all things out of his life that might distract him from his service to God. He wanted to do only what God would have him to do.

"I wanted to be used by the power of the Holy Spirit in the ministry of the Word," Mark says. "I had fully persuaded myself to forget about a life mate. I had left my friendship with Ruth, and I didn't want to get involved any more. I wanted God's best for my life."

Mark was later to learn Huldah was indeed God's best for his life.

The revival meeting lasted five weeks; then Mark went to Vancouver Island for meetings. He could still see Huldah frequently. By the time Mark's sister asked him to return to Toronto for her wedding, he was finding it difficult to leave Huldah. "When I got back to Toronto," he says, "the first thing I wanted to do was return to Vancouver. But that would cost a lot of money, and I didn't have train fare."

The romance had blossomed, however. Huldah's name kept cropping up more frequently in his fervent prayers.

Pastors were still in short supply, because of the war, and Mark was asked to assume another assignment. This time it was at Kenora, on the western edge of Ontario. "I want you to help them out," Dad Buntain told his son.

"If I can get meetings back in British Columbia," he asked his father, "may I return there? Why don't you let Alice and my brother-in-law go to Kenora?"

This little bit of conniving worked. Mark's father agreed that Mark could return to the province of British Columbia where Vancouver is located. But Mark still didn't have train fare.

So Mom Buntain stepped in. She had been keeping boarders to provide finances so Fulton could go to the University of Toronto. She dipped into the savings and gave Mark the fare.

The long train ride seemed interminable, but the exhaustion was forgotten when Mark saw Huldah again. And then, every time Mark had time off between meetings, he went to Vancouver. Mark and Huldah both sought the Lord's guidance and wanted to do God's will.

When Mark had received clearance from his heavenly Father about Huldah, he felt he needed clearance from his earthly dad. While he was thinking of how to approach his father, the phone rang.

Dad Buntain wanted Mark to come quickly to Edmonton, Alberta, and help him with meetings there. There had been difficulty at that time in the Edmonton congregation, and Dan Buntain had been called in to help solve the problems. Mark could help if he would come and preach. Mark agreed reluctantly.

It was winter—very cold and bitter. Dan Buntain always tried to live as cheaply as he could for the benefit of church finances, so he was staying in a small room in a cold house.

When Mark arrived on the train, his father met him at the station and took him to the rooming house. After they had prepared their supper, Mark broached the subject.

"Dad, I want to marry Mr. Alex Monroe's daughter."

"You want to do what?" Mark's father blurted out.

"I want to get married to Huldah Monroe. May I get engaged?"

After a moment, Dad Buntain said, "You know, when I was a young lad back home on Prince Edward Island, I thought I was in love with a girl. One morning I was coming home from the cheese factory where I worked, and she was riding with me in the rig. We passed my father, going the opposite direction in his horse and buggy. When I got home, my dad said, 'Dan, did I see you this morning with that red-faced, freckle-nosed girl?' I decided then I didn't love her after all."

Mark fell silent. He didn't like what he was hearing.

The next morning at breakfast he asked, "Dad, will you come down to the city and help me pick out an engagement ring for Huldah?" His father nodded, and the two went to the Timothy Eaton department store to look at diamonds.

Dan Buntain eyed the rings for a few moments and then whispered to Mark, "Look, why don't you save yourself some money? You come with me."

They left the store and went around the corner to a long row of pawn shops. Mark followed his dad inside.

"May we see some of your diamond rings?" Dan Buntain said.

Several were brought out, and he picked up a large one.

"This is the one," he said to Mark. "Buy this ring cheap, and you can take the stone out, give it to a good jeweler and have him put it in another setting. You'll have a good ring for half the price."

The idea offended Mark's love-smitten heart.

In a rare moment of rebellion, Mark pulled himself up straight and said, "Dad, I'm not giving Huldah any secondhand ring." He turned and walked out of the store.

"We walked home in the bitter cold," Mark recalls. "He said nothing to me all the way home. I thought I would freeze. Finally, when we got to the house I said, 'Dad, I do want to marry Huldah. Please, if you don't want to come with me to buy the ring, just give me permission.' Dad replied, "I'll go with you in the morning.' "

The next day Dan and his son went back into the city to Dinwald's Jewelers. It was the finest jewelry store in the country. They walked up to the counter and Dan Buntain said, "This is my son; he wants to be engaged to a very lovely girl. Will you show him a genuine diamond?"

It was a proud moment for Mark. He knew he had his father's blessing. He came out of the store with an engagement ring in his pocket. He was so afraid he would lose it that he tied it up tightly in his handkerchief, then pinned it to the inside of his trouser pocket.

Mark left Edmonton and began a revival in Colona, British Columbia. It was a great success, with God opening the windows of heaven on that city. The revival lasted for weeks, but Mark was eager to get it over with. He had important business to take care of. There was something else on Mark's mind and he could hardly wait to get down to Vancouver.

Finally the time came.

"I'll never forget that day," he says. "I was going to give Huldah her engagement ring. Her parents knew I had the ring with me. They arranged for us to have supper in a nice restaurant. We went in and were just about to sit at the table when, to my utter surprise, in walked my dear dad. He had changed his plans and had come to Vancouver. He was supposed to be back in eastern Canada.

"What he had never told me was that he knew the Monroe family all the time. In fact, when he came to Vancouver on business, Huldah worked as his secretary. He never told me, nor did he permit her to tell me, because he wanted to be sure Huldah was God's choice and my choice, not his choice for me.

"I was so thankful when I saw him come into the restaurant. I can never thank God enough for my godly, wonderful dad."

And now Mark's dad lay dying of cancer.

Again and again as Mark sat in that westbound plane, his eyes watered up and overflowed. His beloved wife and baby were far behind him, his ministry was suspended in some awful kind of limbo, and his heart ached with grief.

What was happening to him?

9

The Broken Heart

Prayer—deep and fervent—consumed Mark's
trip from Calcutta to Canada. It was a necessity.
Mark's itinerary was terribly tight; if he missed any
of the connections on his twelve-thousand-mile trek,
he would not make Edmonton on time. And every
hour that slipped away brought his father closer to
death.

Trouble began early. Before the first stop, in
Rome, the plane developed engine problems. The
aircraft landed safely, but it would take a major
repair job to get it off the ground again.

The crew knew about Mark's plight—his oddly
stamped ticket had compelled them to ask. They
apologized profusely for the delay, but there was
nothing they could do to speed up the process.

Prayer is truly the secret to Mark's astounding success in India. Dr. Al Holderness, now a member of the board of directors for the Calcutta Mission of Mercy, says, "You almost feel like you are interrupting a conversation between Mark and God when you talk to him. He seems to always be praying."

It is true that Calcutta, with its dying, desperate people, honed Mark's praying to a cutting edge. But even years before India, he knew the value of communication with God.

Mark recalls specifically how he learned to pray.

"When God called me to the ministry, I wanted to go to Bible school. I did enroll. Before I could attend, our country was involved in war. Canada was in the war two years before the USA. Our Winnipeg Rifle Regiment was sent to Hong Kong, where they were trapped by the Japanese and wiped out. Thousands of our boys were killed, and my country began grabbing young men and rushing them to the front with only three months' training.

"I did not finish my education. My doctorate is honorary. You see, I had no one to turn to but God. I had to pray.

"I learned the most important thing to my existence was prayer. God let me know if I would be faithful to Him in this area He would be faithful to meet my needs. God always keeps His bargains.

"Sometimes," Mark admits, "I feel I am Satan's major target. But God has never failed me. I know I can always go to my Lord in prayer. In those beginning years, I learned the value of getting up very early in the morning and praying—so there were no interruptions. It has never been a chore, but it has always been a tremendous blessing.

"I am thankful God does not measure our prayers; He weighs them. I'm sure He doesn't look to see how long a person can pray, but whether we pray.

"I am so grateful that God in His infinite loving kindness showed us the beautiful peace and power there is in prayer. We are nothing in ourselves. We can do nothing by ourselves, but thank God all things are possible when we believe."

Mark has learned the power of *continual* prayer. He prays as he drives his car. He prays at work.

"God is pleased if we keep in a spirit of prayer," he says. "I have found if I want God's touch in my life, I cannot compromise. I have discovered I dare not allow Satan to bring even the smallest smutty thing into my imagination. I cannot allow anything discolored to come to my thinking. I have to walk with God. If I do not walk with Him, I cannot expect His blessing. Without prayer, I could not stay in Calcutta."

And so it was natural for Mark to pray when his homebound plane broke down in Rome.

"I do want to get home," he prayed earnestly in the terminal building, thinking of his dying father. "Can you please help these dear people get the plane fixed?"

Within a few minutes the crew returned.

"It's fixed," they reported. "Be ready to go in twenty minutes."

Miraculously, Mark made his connections in both London and Montreal, and finally touched down in Edmonton.

Fulton met Mark at the airport. It was bitterly cold, and the young preacher raced to the ramp and threw an overcoat around his big brother. The tears froze on their faces as they embraced. Fulton had begun his young adult life in rebellion against the godly father who now lay dying in a hospital bed. As a teen he resented his father's frequent absences and the ministry that made them necessary. This godly heritage had been too stifling for fun-loving Fulton.

"Dad and mom were firm with the family altar," Mark recalls. "We had five family members, and I remember there were five Bibles on a small shelf by our table. The large one was dad's, then came mother's, next was Alice's little Bible, mine was the fourth, and Fulton's was the last.

"Twice a day these Bibles came down from the shelf, and our family read and prayed together. When we were old enough, we each read—and then each child prayed aloud. It was a wonderful heritage."

Fulton would have disagreed back then. The strong will and tenacity that have helped Mark last in India were also trademarks of Fulton's personality from the start.

He felt cramped with all the religious exercise, and, while he did not openly rebel, he bided his time until he could leave home and do what he wanted to do.

Fulton had ambitions. He would not be a miserable preacher with a miserable pittance called a salary. No, he would be a doctor, make lots of money and enjoy life. He waited.

Although Mark managed well during his dad's absences, Fulton needed more attention than he received. So while Fulton had great love and respect for his father, he resolved never to become a preacher.

Fulton entered the University of Toronto to begin his premedical studies. Being athletic and sociable, he soon made friends. The conservative Buntain family would not have approved of some of them, but what they didn't know wouldn't hurt them, Fulton reasoned.

Before long, Fulton stopped going to church, and his commitment for Christ vanished. Rumors began to circulate about the preacher's son being "wild," unlike the rest of the dedicated family.

Dan and Kathleen were heartbroken. Alice and Mark shared that sorrow as they watched their bright and warm brother throwing his life away in sin.

Mark vividly recalls those terrible times.

"My father was so conscious of his son's waywardness when he preached at conferences and camp meetings. Here he was telling others how to live, and his own boy was out in sin.

"My mother taught in the Bible school in Toronto. But she was so concerned about Fulton that she promised God she would fast and pray much of the week until he was saved. She came home from teaching school and went to bed, unable to do her household chores because of weakness from her fastings. I often heard her weep and pray for Fulton in the long hours of the night."

By this time Mark was an evangelist. He and Huldah were married, and both were praying for Fulton. Meanwhile, the prodigal Fulton attended the University of Toronto Medical School and worked at a funeral home to make ends meet. His weekends were spent pursuing pleasure and letting off steam.

About this time, Dan Buntain decided he should resign his national post as general superintendent of the Assemblies of God in Canada to take a pastorate in Edmonton, Alberta. Fulton decided to change universities so he could be nearer home and save money.

Mark was the guest speaker in his dad's church when Fulton came home.

"I will never forget the weekend my brother arrived in Edmonton," Mark recalls. "Dad had sent him money for the ticket. He came off the train and was so worldly in his dress. He had been smoking. The smell of tobacco was on his clothes. He came into the house, sat down sullenly, and said to me, 'You might as well worship that incandescent light bulb as worship God.'

"My heart was broken. I said, 'Fulton, you know better than that!' I got up and walked out." But even in the depths of bitter rebellion Fulton went to hear his brother preach out of family loyalty. He sat sulking under the balcony on the ground floor.

Mark preached on Pontius Pilate. When he finished, he looked back at his brother—and his heart broke for Fulton.

He left the pulpit, walked to the back, reached over several people, and put his hand on Fulton's shoulder, pleading, "Fulton, come, give your life to Christ."

Then without waiting, Mark turned around and walked toward the altar. He knew his brother was following.

Fulton knelt down by the front bench. Dan Buntain left the platform and knelt beside the wayward son. He kissed him, just as the prodigal's father had done in the Bible story. Dan, usually an unemotional person, was so filled with gratitude that he wept openly that night.

Still the struggle was not over. The next Tuesday Mark went into a small room to pray in preparation for the service. He felt someone else enter that room. He could tell the person was kneeling nearby.

The man began to cry. Mark opened his eyes and saw it was Fulton.

Mark knelt down beside his brother and asked, "What's wrong?"

"I don't want to give in," Fulton said, "because if I do, I will have to preach. I don't want to preach."

"Fulton, you will never be happy until you do," Mark said softly.

Mark closed his meeting that night in Edmonton, and his next meeting started in Spokane, Washington. When he arrived, the pastor handed Mark a special delivery letter from Dad Buntain. Mark fumbled it open anxiously and read a simple note: "Pray. Fulton is on his way to Central Bible College."

CBC was very difficult for Fulton. He was still worldly. His new friends there were not as good an influence as they should have been. Fulton was finding it difficult to adjust. For several weeks his new faith floundered.

Then the godly W.I. Evans—who had changed Alice's life—again stepped in.

He called Fulton to his office and said, "Fulton, I know your father. I know your sister. I know your brother. The trouble with you is you don't have enough responsibility. I know you are a first-year student, but starting next Sunday you will be pastor of one of our mission churches. You go and get your music ready and get your sermon, because they will now be your responsibility."

Fulton, a little awed by Evans, did not know how to object. So he started preaching.

One Sunday morning, after a service at his tiny Missouri mission, someone called for Fulton. He was told an old lady down the road was dying, and she was calling for a preacher.

Fulton panicked, but there was no one else who could go.

He went to the bedside of the dying woman and led her to Jesus before she passed away. It was the first soul he had led to Christ.

This had a tremendous impact on Fulton's life. Shortly afterward he wired his mother that he had been baptized with the Holy Spirit.

All during the years Fulton was at CBC, Mark and Huldah traveled as evangelists. Mark kept encouraging Fulton to come and travel with them when he finished school.

Evangelism was big business in those days. Billy Graham and Oral Roberts were constantly in the news headlines, and it seemed there were big crowds and rallies everywhere.

Most of the young would-be preachers in Fulton's dormitory dreamed of owning huge gospel tents and gaining national recognition. But Fulton only wanted to travel with Mark.

Graduation day finally came, and all the Buntains drove from Canada to Springfield, Missouri, so they could witness Fulton's graduation. He would not be a doctor of bodies, but of souls.

After graduation, Mark and Huldah asked Fulton to join them in a revival campaign at Ed and Alice's church in Auburn, Washington. It was a wonderful week of family reunion and rejoicing for the Buntains.

Mark always accepted any invitation to preach, regardless of the church size. He had promised a young preacher that the team would go to his town for meetings and help him out, although only a few people would show up. The church was located in a tiny mountain logging community, and that Saturday night the three Buntains drove up and down Highway 99 looking for the village. No one seemed to know where it was. Finally, quite late, they found the place.

The pastor also supported himself working as a logger. The Buntains were all to stay in a single room at the back of the church.

"My brother had spent three years at CBC with roommates who dreamed of big-time evangelism," Mark remembers. "He was bewildered when he saw what evangelism was really like.

"When the pastor showed us the room, my brother settled back into a large chair. Behind his head was a hole in the wall. My brother asked the pastor, 'What's this hole?' 'Oh,' the pastor nonchalantly said, 'that's just a bullet hole. A man in the community doesn't like his wife coming to church. The other night she was in prayer meeting and he came in and shot at her.'

"When the pastor left, my brother asked, 'Is this the best you can do? After all of these years as an evangelist, you mean you end up here?' "

What Fulton did not know was Mark's next meeting was set for one of America's largest churches. But in spite of everything, the revival in that little logging town on Highway 99 was a great success. Fulton preached with Mark, and several were saved.

The team packed up and headed to Minneapolis, Minnesota. They had an agreement that Fulton would preach Sunday mornings and Mark would preach Sunday nights. When they arrived at the massive Minnesota church, Fulton was impressed. Apparently evangelism wasn't so bad after all.

But when Fulton stood up to preach on Sunday morning, Mark remembers, "That big crowd scared him silly. He soon discovered you need the Lord in all circumstances. Big-time evangelism isn't as big-time as it looks if you don't have God to help you."

God blessed the meeting in Minnesota. There were many miracles of healing, and a number of people were saved. In fact, it was that meeting that caught the eye of a nationally known evangelist. The prominent preacher came to Mark and asked him to join his ministries.

It was a tempting offer. This evangelist was often in the headlines. There was, without a doubt, a touch of God on this man's life.

"He begged me to come and join him," Mark recalls. "I remember standing out on the sidewalk in front of the church. It was snowing hard, and he pleaded, 'Mark, come.' He had a great city-wide meeting planned, and he wanted me. But God would not let me go.

"I thank God. Fulton and I stayed together until I realized it was time for him to be on his own. Then I told him, 'You must do your own preaching. You must take your own meetings.' "

Mark talks about Fulton through tears.

"God has had His hand on Fulton's wonderful, profitable life. When I visit Tacoma now and see him pastoring that great First Assembly of God church, with its two thousand seats completely filled on Sunday morning, I can only look back with great gratitude.

"My brother is by far a greater preacher than I. I will never be able to do for God what He has done—and is doing."

10

I Have to Go Back

Mark and Fulton embraced at the frigid Edmonton airport and then went straight to the hospital, where their father was slipping away from them. There, Mark learned that his dad was indeed in critical condition. He was full of cancer and nothing would help. His dad was going to die.

Mark sat by his bedside day after day, helpless. Every new day, he watched his father's life slowly ebb from him.

Four grieving weeks dragged by.

But cancer is an unpredictable disease, and Mark's dad fought it ferociously. Finally he told the doctors, "If I am going to die, let me die at home." The elder Buntain lived across the street from the hospital, so the doctors agreed.

At home, Dad Buntain began to improve slightly.

One morning, the old man called Mark to his bedside.

"Son, it was always my desire that you carry on my work here in Canada," he said. "But now I know as long as there is one soul in India without Christ, you must go back. God has called you to Calcutta."

With his father's future in question, Mark began preparing to follow that final piece of advice. He would return to Calcutta.

Although British Airways had helped Mark, he still had to pay them for the fare. He had promised he would send them funds for his ticket as soon as he arrived in Edmonton. It was only a couple of days after his arrival that Mark learned how faithful God was in providing this need.

On the Sunday before Mark left Calcutta, an evangelist in an Edmonton church stood up to say to the congregation, "Let us bring Mark home, since his father is so ill."

The congregation responded beautifully, and gave their offering toward his fare. Then Mark was asked to drop by the church office, and there a secretary handed him an envelope.

"Mark," she said, "here is the money for your air passage home."

When he counted the money it was $150 short. Mark was deeply appreciative, but he didn't know how he would get the rest.

"Jesus, I haven't had to ask you for money for a

long time," Mark prayed later, at his father's home, "but I need $150. Will you please help me?"

In the afternoon mail a letter arrived from a lady Mark did not know.

"I was in a meeting where you were speaking," she wrote. "For two weeks God had been dealing with me about my salvation, but I was resisting, saying, 'I can't live this Christian life.' I had made up my mind I could not be a Christian.

"But I thought it would be best to tell God no in church. So I came to your meeting to just say, 'No, Lord, I can't live this kind of life.'

"Then, as I listened to your message, my heart was moved. Still I did not go forward. You walked back to the pulpit after you had finished preaching and said, 'I believe God is giving someone in this place one more chance. Will you come to Christ?'

"I was that person. If you had not walked back to the pulpit and said what you did, I would have been a lost soul. Instead of saying no to God I surrendered. Will you accept my gift of $150 in appreciation?"

During those four weeks in Edmonton, Mark had left his dad's side only on a few occasions. One was to attend a Wednesday afternoon ladies' prayer meeting. Mark fell on his knees by the piano to ask God to heal his father. But, as Mark's knees touched the floor, God broke his heart for India. He cannot remember how long he prayed, but he sobbed and sobbed.

When Mark stood he told the ladies, "I have not been praying for my father, I have been praying for India."

They already knew that. They could see the divine intervention in Mark's life by the Holy Spirit, fulfilling Paul's word: "Likewise the Spirit also helpeth our infirmities: for we know not what we should pray for as we ought: but the Spirit itself maketh intercession for us with groanings which cannot be uttered" (Rom. 8:26).

Never again would Mark doubt his calling to Calcutta.

Finally Mark left his dying father to return to India. Dan Buntain wanted it that way. Still, it was one of the hardest moments of Mark's life.

His mother saw him off at the airport and pleaded with him.

"Mark, is there no other way? Can't someone else go to Calcutta? We need you here so badly."

But he could not stay. The mother embraced her son, perhaps for the first time realizing the full significance of her vow to dedicate this child of promise.

Returning to Calcutta, Mark saw the city through different eyes. His heart was broken for India. He now knew he could do something about the death around him. God had called him here, and here he would spend his life.

The Buntains continued as evangelists throughout India for the next few months. Then, while preaching a revival in Madras, Mark received a phone call from his mother.

"Dad just collapsed in the back yard," she said. "He is back in the hospital. He will not make it. Can you please come home?"

Under normal circumstances the mission board does not allow two journeys so close together, even in the event of a close relative's death. But because Mark's first agreement was to minister for one year, it was time to go home.

"God looked ahead," Mark says, "and saw that in one year I would be needed back home. So I was able to return. If anyone had ever told me I would be able to help arrange my own father's funeral and help my broken-hearted mother, I would not have believed them. God is so good."

Mom Buntain was deeply grieved. She had received cables from missionaries saying, "Hold on, Sister Buntain. God's on the throne. Brother Buntain is going through the valley, but he will be all right."

Many were praying the very night Dad Buntain died, and some people were sure God was saying He would raise up Dan Buntain.

But God chose to take the old soldier home. Just before 11:00 P.M., Dan Buntain joined his Lord around the throne.

Mark interrupted the tenacious prayer group insisting on his dad's healing to tell them the news.

Dan Buntain was a well-known figure in Canada

117

and all the press reported his passing. Hundreds mourned his homegoing, especially the poor of the city who had been fed, clothed and comforted in the ministry of Dan and Kathleen Buntain. The Buntains had always believed in "putting their sermons into shoe leather."

A few weeks after the funeral, Mark was at the church praying when an overwhelming burden for India came on him. He finished praying and went to Huldah.

"I have to go back to India."

They had only been home three months, but Mark knew it was time to go back.

"We haven't even unpacked our things," Huldah said. But she too knew when God spoke they must listen.

Immediately Mark telephoned the Foreign Missions Department and talked to the field director.

"Can I go back to India?" he asked.

"Mark," the missions executive said, "I have just returned from Rev. Noel Perkin's office and we were wondering what to do. We have so much trouble in India, and we were wondering if you would go back. I was going to call you."

Arrangements were made, and the Buntains returned almost immediately to their adopted country.

It would be six years before they saw North America again.

Mark harbored no illusions about his ability to penetrate the spiritual consciousness of the vast Indian nation. He knew traditionally the people of India had resisted most efforts of evangelism, even though some of Christendom's greatest heroes had laid down their lives there to plant the cross of Christ. In fact, St. Thomas is said to have been the first missionary ever to preach on India's shores. After the Resurrection and Ascension of Christ this former "doubting disciple" is said to have traveled to ancient India—then called Hindustan—to make converts for the Christ he loved.

While Thomas's trip to India cannot be historically documented, Mark did know great men of missions had tried to penetrate the darkness of India ever since the second century. Pantaenus, founder and president of the world's first missionary training school, the Catechetical School at Alexandria, preached in India for a decade, from 180 to 190 A.D. This great Alexandrian preacher traveled to India in response to messengers who had been sent out from India with an appeal for Christian teaching. He found a few Christians in India who possessed a Gospel of Matthew, and he discovered about 350 flourishing churches throughout that vast land.

Little else was done to take Christ to the truly lost subcontinent until Catholic priest Francis Xavier moved through the southern coasts of the country, making converts to the Catholic church, in the middle 1500s. His restless spirit drove Xavier so much that, during his brief but intense missionary career, he is said to have planted the cross in fifty-two different kingdoms, preached through 9,000 miles of territory, and baptized over a million souls.

Xavier often had night visions, seeing the world conquered for Christ. He would awaken shouting, "Yet more, O my God! Yet more!"

The dedicated priest died of a raging fever on the little island of St. John, off China's southeastern coast. Those last hours of earthly life were spent looking toward the impenetrable Chinese nation crying, "O rock, rock! When will thou open to my Master?"

Two hundred years passed, and another wave of evangelism inevitably washed on India's shores. The Danish-Halle Mission to India was formed, sending Bartholomew Ziegenbalg and Henry Plutschau as the first Protestant missionaries to reach the land of the Hindu. Although the King of Denmark had permitted the two missionaries to go to India, the two-faced king also sent orders to block their effort in deference to the hostile Danish East India Company of merchants. Ironically the king's courier, with this message to India's Danish governor, traveled on the same ship as the two men of God.

Despite opposition, the missionaries were able to establish a beachhead for Christ in India, and within three years had translated the New Testament into one of the native Indian languages. This had never been done before in India.

Ten months after their arrival they had baptized five adults, and a few months later nine other Hindus turned to Jesus Christ.

The Danish-Halle Mission later sent a third missionary to India. He was Christian Frederic Schwartz, who would become founder of the native Christian church of that land.

Schwartz mastered many of the dialects of India and became so proficient in Hindu literature and mythology that he extended the influence of Christ to the regal courts of the ruling Mohammedan princes. Schwartz was an untiring worker for the Lord, establishing many churches and schools for Christ.

By this time England started to exert its powerful arm of influence in India and pushed the Danes aside. But Schwartz had become so respected by both sides he was the only man through whom they would negotiate. Also, the Mohammedan princes, when forced to deal with the British, demanded Schwartz as mediator saying, "Send me the Christian. He will not deceive me."

When Schwartz died in 1798, the native Prince of Tanjore, along with the East India Company, erected a huge monument to him. But perhaps the best abiding monument came when the Moslems and Hindus, in spite of their religion and culture, insisted on being the chief mourners at his funeral.

One prince even erected a massive marble monument for Schwartz and laboriously wrote the epitaph himself. It was the first known English verse to be written by an Indian: "Firm was thou, humble and wise, honest and pure, free from disguise; father of orphans, the widow's support; comfort in sorrow of every sort. To the beknighted dispenser of light, doing and pointing to that which is right. Blessing to princes, to people, to me; May I, my Father, be worthy of thee."

But without a doubt the prince of all Indian missionaries was William Carey. This cobbler from Northamptonshire, England, mastered Latin, Greek, Hebrew, French, Dutch and a number of Indian languages. His heart burned that the lost might come to Christ. This was an unpopular concept in the early 1800s, and Carey had to overcome tremendous opposition to carry out his mission. As a young man, while still earning his living as a cobbler, Carey hung a large map of the world in his shop with statistics and Scripture verses. He often looked up from his work and prayed passionately that God would save the lost world.

When Carey entered the ministry, he attended a ministerial meeting at Nottingham. Brashly, the young cleric rose and proposed to that august body, "The duty of Christians is to attempt the spread of the gospel among the heathen nations."

Boos and catcalls from his colleagues drowned out his voice. He was finally silenced when the moderator rose and said sharply, "Young man, sit down. When God pleases to convert the heathen, He will do it without your aid or mine."

That statement was only partially true. God did do it without the moderator's aid, but not without the aid of the young Carey.

Carey's shadow still falls far over the land of India. His first years there were hard, but during his long and fruitful ministry he literally changed the complexion and customs of that country. Carey is singly credited with abolishing the *suttee* rite of burning widows on the funeral pyres of their husbands. More than that, this great man of faith translated God's Word into the languages of the Indians. Also through his influence, the government was forced to pass laws prohibiting throwing children into the Ganges for sacrifice to Hindu gods. In his forty-one years of sacred service, Dr. Carey left India and the church his eternal debtors. It was he who introduced to the Church that great axiom: "Attempt great things for God. Expect great things from God."

Henry Martyn, Alexander Huff, Reginald Heber, and Adoniram Judson all followed. Judson arrived in Calcutta only to be ordered out by the despotic and God-hating East India Company. Undaunted, he left for Burma and became God's chosen apostle there.

John Scudder came as India's first medical missionary. For thirty-six years he labored for the

Master and left India a large family of missionary children and grandchildren who would follow and serve Christ on her shores to the fifth generation.

When Dr. and Mrs. Clough came, there was a wave of great revival. On one day in 1878, this powerful Baptist preacher baptized over 2,000 converts. Another 8,000 were added to the church within the next six weeks.

That was a turning point for the Indian church—and a crack in the door to gospel-hardened India. Christianity was making strides. Then suddenly, the door was slammed shut by a new spirit of nationalism sweeping through all of India just as Mark Buntain arrived.

It was this backdrop of missions history that Mark understood. He knew the field was hard and the laborers few. He also knew God would help him penetrate the thick darkness of India's night.

Nevertheless, Calcutta was the breeding place of rebellion when Mark moved his little family there. They had entered the flaming, red-hot mouth of hell.

Mark and Huldah Buntain.

Ron Hembree, Vernon Mc Lellen, Mark on PTL Club with Jim and Tammy Bakker.

Van PTL gave to Mark.

Mark visits with Jimmy Swaggart.

School children line up for classes.

Children of Calcutta.

Love in Action.

School boys enjoying their lunch.

Patiently waiting for their daily bread.

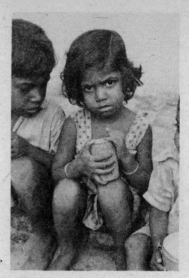

"Unto the least of these."

A young mother and her baby.

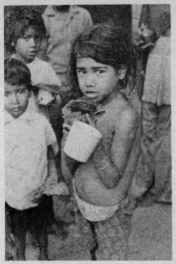

God's provision wrapped in love.

Anticipation.

Spoons full of hope to satisfy.

School provides food for body, soul and spirit.

11

No Time to Quit

About the time Joseph was sold into Egyptian slavery by his jealous brothers, Aryan invaders were sweeping over the blasting hot plains of India, robbing, raping, and plundering. These "foreign devils" subjected the docile Indians to a caste system in an attempt to get an iron grip on their minds.

Frequently throughout her troubled history India has been subjected to invasions and rule by foreign powers. Alexander the Great sought to conquer India. The mighty Moguls set up their palatial empire headquarters in Agra and for centuries ruled the meek and spiritually weakened Indian people, introducing the Moslem religion to that Hindu country. Later the Portuguese came, and finally the British Raj.

Generally, the mild-mannered Indians took the invaders in good stride. However, a frail little man changed all that when he captured the imagination of his countrymen and brought the mighty British Empire to its knees. He was Mahatma Gandhi, the "great soul" who became the father of nationalism in modern India. To India's masses he was a Hindu saint. To England and Winston Churchill he was a fraud who always stopped short of his "fasts to death" and wielded great political power. With Gandhi's "Salt march to the sea" and his frequent fastings, the little bald-headed leader wrenched control of India from the English and placed it firmly in the unprepared hands of his own people.

However, Gandhi spawned a nationalism that cut both ways. Without a doubt it was good India had her independence. But even in peaceful revolutions, the new leaders often throw the baby out with the bath water. In their determined efforts for self-government, the Indian people began to despise and resist anything "Western." Thus, anti-Americanism and anti-Western feeling grew—until the very life of the struggling Indian church was threatened.

Calcutta was teeming with nationalism when Mark and Huldah returned. People of the Bengal Province where Calcutta is located, have a saying: "What Calcutta thinks today, all of India will think tomorrow." The very heart of nationalism was centered in Calcutta. The city was virtually seething in rebellion and anger when the Buntains came back from America.

Anything Western was to be abhorred. And this nationalistic spirit caught on in the churches. Try as they might, the missionaries could not impress the Indian people that Christianity was not "Western" and their efforts were not designed to "Americanize" the Indian, but to convert him to Jesus Christ. In that seething cauldron of confusion, many national church leaders spoke of breaking away from the American-controlled missions boards.

Feelings were running high. Tensions mounted. Missions boards were reluctant to leave after having invested hundreds of thousands of dollars—as well as the lives of their missionaries—in India. But many leaders in the national Indian church resented the intrusion from these foreign representatives.

A long, slow exodus of missionaries began. Many gave up and returned to their homeland. They had been beaten and broken by India. Some others merely waited out their terms until retirement and busied themselves hunting tigers and retreating to the Himalayas from the hot, sweaty plains. The new Indian government began pressing the remaining missionaries to abandon their posts and leave the Indians to their own religion and culture. Even in the tiny mission work where Mark was assigned as director, there was a militant spirit of nationalism. The Indians resented Mark's presence. Those were hard and dark days for the gospel.

Mark and Huldah threw all they had into the Calcutta work. Almost every night, Mark met with his Indian board. The conclaves were often tense and angry. Meetings lasted until the small hours of the morning. Usually, little was resolved.

The Indian nationals were standing their ground. Mark was not wanted. The local people would accept funds he brought from the States, but they wanted nothing of his control. Everything he did, they said, was "Americanism."

One thing in Mark's favor was his Canadian birthright. As a Canadian he was not under as much suspicion as he would have been if he were from the United States.

Still, he had American money and he was a foreigner.

After weeks of fruitless meetings, the field director for India came to Calcutta. This head of all American missionaries met with Mark and the board. When the tense meeting finally adjourned at 2:00 A.M., the issues were still unresolved.

"The Assemblies of God have tried for fifty years to get a break in this city," the frustrated director told Mark. "Nothing has worked. Mark, if you and Huldah want to go back home, I'll give you the money for your fare tonight. I don't blame you. Nothing can be done here."

Again that familiar inner voice spoke to Mark, and he said to his superior, "Now is no time to quit."

A few weeks later, after much prayer and fasting,

Mark called the rebellious board into his office. With boldness which came from spending hours with God, Mark gave them a flat ultimatum.

"Gentlemen, I don't care what you do. But I will tell you what I am going to do. We are here to stay. Now, if you want to be part of the team, you can. If you don't, then you can leave right now. I am staying in Calcutta, and we are going to have a church here."

Such a direct approach is foreign to the graces of India's culture. But Mark had been moved by the Spirit of God, and the national leaders sensed his determination.

It was the turning point. Slowly, each rebellious leader came into line, and the team meshed together in unity and spirit. The first and most important victory was won.

Mark and his little church held their meetings in a tent on an open lot. It was the only place available and the property was owned by Moslems.

Moslems are fiercely loyal to their religion and usually hate Christians intensely. Even today in India, when a Moslem comes to Christ, he often risks death. His family feels obligated to kill the apostate one, lest he influence others in the Moslem community. Although this feeling is dissipating somewhat, especially in the cities, Moslem sentiment against Christianity is still strong.

So it came as no surprise when a few weeks later the Moslem property owner evicted Mark and his tent from the property. The only other place available for the tiny struggling church was above a night club on one of the city's main streets. The place was filthy, but Mark and his men cleaned it up and started holding services every day. People often joked and said, "You can find your way to heaven upstairs and find your way to hell downstairs." No one can say how many found their way to hell downstairs, but many lost souls began to learn about Christ in the small quarters of the "upper room."

Before long, space in Mark's little church was totally inadequate. Meetings were jammed full of new people being saved and wanting to join the new church. Mark looked everywhere, but in that crowded city no other meeting places were available. He knew he would have to build.

With the strong anti-Western feeling in the government, it would be an almost impossible task. No new church had been built in Calcutta for the past century.

But Mark began to look for property anyway.

He found a small empty lot on Royd Street that had been reclaimed from a swamp. He checked its ownership and discovered that an old Moslem man owned the property and lived next-door to it.

Mark looked him up and got a flat refusal. He would never sell the property to any Christian, the man declared.

Undaunted, Mark went back every day—until in a rage the old Moslem screamed in the missionary's face, "Don't you ever come back here again!"

Once again Mark found himself in that familiar position—up against the impossible. He took his characteristic action—he prayed. He called several members of his church together that very night, and they began to bombard heaven, asking God to change the old Moslem's mind. They agreed together that the impossible would be done.

After a couple hours of prayer, Mark felt victory. Since he was no longer welcome in the Moslem's home, he sent one of the prayer group to ask the man again. As soon as the courier entered the house, the old Moslem sighed resignedly.

"Tell Rev. Buntain to come and see me tomorrow," the man said. "I will sell." The amazed Christian dashed back with the news.

The next day Mark was again at the old Moslem's home. After they were seated, the man looked sharply at Mark. "Sir, I will sell you the property," he said, "if you can get my tax problems cleared up. I owe 85,000 rupees in back taxes, and I will not get out of my chair to solve this problem. But if you solve it, I will sell you the land."

Mark knew the mandate was not an easy one. In Bengal, Calcutta's province, Hindus control the government. Moslems are a small minority, and generally not liked by the Hindus. So, when a Moslem gets into tax trouble, Hindu officials often attempt to prosecute to the full extent of the law. A Moslem is given little consideration, and his case drags on for years. The courts seem to want to drain the resources of the Moslems.*

Mark was on the spot. He could not have the land unless he met the old Moslem's demands.

"I will take care of your tax troubles," Mark heard himself say to the old man. But he knew it would be far easier to say than to do.

Mark went straight to the government office in charge of taxes. When he told the official what he wanted, the man rudely interrupted.

"His problems are none of your business. We will not even discuss the case with you."

But when Mark has a directive from the Lord, he is more tenacious than a bulldog after a bone. Every day he returned to the tax office. Every day he received the same answer.

Finally, after weeks of this routine, the official asked Mark, "Why do you keep coming back? You know our answer."

"Because Jesus Christ is a living Lord," Mark replied, "and you will see one day that He will help me."

---

*India's independence splintered the nation of Pakistan. Pakistan is predominantly Moslem, while India is Hindu. During that terrible time, hundreds of thousands of Indians were relocated, with Hindus in Pakistan being forced to relocate in India, and the Moslems in India being shuffled to Pakistan. Bitter and bloody fightings broke out between the two religions. Trainloads of Hindus were stopped and slaughtered by the Moslems. Hindus retaliated by murdering and maiming thousands of Moslems. Blood ran deep in the streets. The carnage was so great that buzzards sat on rooftops waiting to feast on the dead and murdered Indians. Much of the animosity now is part of the bitter past. East Pakistan is no longer, but now is known as Bangladesh.

The Hindu exploded in anger, shaking his fist in Mark's face and screamed, "You will never build a church in Calcutta as long as I live and have anything to do with it."

Several weeks after his first visit to the tax office, Mark again stood in the long line waiting to see the tax official. The building was jammed with impatient Indians. As Mark waited, a young man bumped into him.

The youth spun around and said, "Why, Rev. Buntain, what are you doing here?"

Mark told him he was waiting to see the tax official, and the man said, "Come with me to my office."

Mark followed the youth into a comfortable office, still not knowing who he was. Apparently the man knew Mark, but Mark could not remember where they had met.

When Mark was seated, the man dismissed himself.

"Just a moment and I will return."

Within a few minutes, the youth was back.

"Rev. Buntain, you don't know who I am," he said. "But my wife was dying of tuberculosis. I brought her to your church and you prayed for her. She was healed instantly and has been completely dismissed from the doctor's care.

"I have just learned you are trying to get a tax problem cleared up. I am a tax officer, and although I do not live in Calcutta, I am here to oversee their work. Let me help you fill out all the forms and show you how you can present your case to court."

With the forms filled out, Mark was now a step closer. The lengthy court procedure came next. Mark then started going to court every day to resolve the tax problem.

Finally one of the tax lawyers yelled at him.

"Sir, I will personally see to it that you will never build a church in Calcutta! We don't want your kind here! Why don't you leave us alone and go back to America? As long as I live, you will never build a church!"

About that time, Mark received a cable from the United States. A number of young Americans had raised $20,000 to build an evangelistic center in Calcutta. If he could get his tax problems cleared within the next few months, that money would be available to him.

Mark rejoiced because he felt another step closer to victory. But as the months dragged by, Mark received a second cable from his missions board. They were giving the $20,000 to another mission field, since it now appeared that Mark would never be able to build a Calcutta church. But Mark refused to give up.

Two years passed, and still the court case was delayed. The little upper-room church bulged, and the property owner became more irritated by the constant trek of people upstairs. He was pressing Mark to abandon the rented room. A crisis was developing.

Frustrated by the impasse, knowing God had directed him so far, Mark decided to take a brash step of faith. He had just received word that two Assemblies of God executives, the Reverend Bert Webb and the Reverend J.R. Flower, would be traveling to India for an inspection trip of the mission field. This had never happened before. Mark seized the rare opportunity.

He went to the print shop close to the church and made up posters to put all over Calcutta. The posters announced that there would be a ground-breaking ceremony on the Royd Street property for a new Calcutta church on the same Sunday the American church officials would be there.

It was an audacious move, insane by all human standards. The court case had not even come up. The tax troubles had no hope of being resolved. The case could drag on for years. But Mark felt this move was dictated by God.

When the posters were printed and distributed, Mark took one to the court. While he was there, he happened to meet an old lawyer who he learned was highly esteemed in the government. This greatly respected attorney had written all the tax laws for Bengal after their independence. The old lawyer took an immediate liking to Mark.

"Sir, I have a problem," Mark said meekly.

"What is it, son?" the attorney asked.

Mark showed him the poster and said, "Sir, my

mission board has entrusted to me the greatest chore of my life. If I fail, I will lose face. Can you help me?"

Mark explained the long fight over taxes and the frustration he had encountered.

When he finished, the lawyer said, "Reverend, you be here at 10:00 A.M. on Saturday, and I will have this case finished in twenty minutes."

Saturday Mark was in court early. He paced the floor waiting for the old lawyer. Even Mark was having a hard time believing the lawyer could solve the case in twenty minutes, no matter who or how good he was.

But the attorney showed up on time and the court opened. Then Mark's heart sank. The prosecutor, it turned out, was the same man who had shaken his fist in Mark's face.

When the court opened Mark began to speak up. But the old lawyer placed his hand on Mark's knee and whispered, "Now, Reverend, you keep quiet. I'll do the talking. You go across the street and tell the clerk at the filing court to keep his office open an extra twenty-five minutes. Give him twenty-five rupees and say we will be over to file for the property by then."

Mark obeyed, and the clerk of the property court agreed to stay open. True to his word, the old lawyer came to the office twenty-five minutes later with the tax problem resolved. Mark signed the deed for the Royd Street property at 2:30 that afternoon.

Right on schedule, Mark had his ground-breaking

ceremony. The two executives from America spoke, smiled, and dug shovels into the swampy ground, not knowing Mark had actually obtained the property less then twenty-four hours before.

While Mark had the property, he still did not have a church on it or the money to build one.

Again he prayed. Within days a cable arrived from an attorney in Kansas City, Missouri, who said his client had just died and willed $20,000 to build a church in Calcutta. Could Mark use the money? Yes, praise the Lord, he could!

Although Mark had now been in Calcutta almost three years, he still did not know the business community. His world was with the common people; he never circulated with the very rich. So when he had to find a builder for the new church, he had no idea whom to see.

He sat down one night and drew out a rough floor plan of what he felt the church should be like, and then set off to find a contractor. Rumor had it that the finest builder in Calcutta was an old British firm called McClintock, Burns and Company.

Mark decided to pay them a visit. After all, God deserved the best.

When Mark was ushered into the prestigious offices of the contracting firm he met first with the architect. Showing the architect his floor plans, Mark went on to explain his vision for a large church building on Royd Street. The architect listened and then asked a key question.

"How much money do you have to spend?"

"I have only $20,000," Mark replied.

The architect threw the floor plans back to Mark. "Impossible," he spat out. "It is ridiculous to even think about a building such as yours at that amount."

Mark sat silently until the architect became uncomfortable. Finally, to get support in the silence the young man said, "Let me call another architect and get his opinion."

Within moments a second architect came in. He told Mark the same thing.

Just then an elderly, distinguished man walked by their desks.

"What's the matter, fellows?" he asked. The architects told him that Mark wanted to build a church, but his available capital was far too low. It simply could not be done.

The man beckoned Mark into his office.

Settling back into his overstuffed chair, the old man told Mark he was the managing director of the firm.

He leaned across the desk and said, "Reverend, I am retiring and moving out of Calcutta. I have built many buildings here, but I would like to leave knowing that the very last thing I did was build a church.

"If you will not tell the community, I will build your church for the $20,000. That won't even cover the material costs, but I will do it."

"Sir," Mark said, "there is one more slight

problem."

"What's that?" the old man asked, peering suspiciously.

"It has to be finished in six months. We have just received an eviction notice from our rented hall, and we have to be out by Christmas."

"Well, that does pose a problem," the contractor said. "Let's go talk with our engineers."

Mark followed the contractor to the engineer's office. After they explained the problem, the contractor said, "Now, tell me if we can get this building done by Christmas. Don't lie to this preacher. If you say it will be done, I want no excuses. It must be done."

"Reverend, get your Christmas Day sermon ready," the engineer said. "You will be in your church on Christmas Day."

From the moment excavation began, the contractor ran into trouble. The land on Royd Street had been reclaimed from a swamp, and it was wet and mushy. The building would have to be set on pile drivings, and this was not in the original agreement. The contractor put in the pilings anyway, and absorbed the costs himself.

Hundreds of workers swarmed over the property, and daily the building grew.

In late fall, the contractor visited the site. Delays had created problems. At that moment, he called in his crews from other jobs and ran the work twenty-four hours a day so he could keep his word to

Mark.

On December 25, 1959, the congregation had its first service in the new building. It was the first house of worship to be built in "the city of the dreadful night" in one hundred years. Already Mark had wrenched one victory from the goddess of death and planted a burning torch of hope in her sea of darkness.

12

Angel of Mercy

From the day the doors opened on Royd Street, it was apparent that Calcutta's new church would have a unique ministry. There are other churches in Calcutta. In fact, one of the world's most beautiful Gothic structures stands in the midst of the city's decay. Built two centuries ago by the British, that church is really a museum that memorializes the many skirmishes between the English invaders and the Indians. Throughout every hall and on all the walls are plaques in ponderous English, telling of angry battles and gruesome deaths.

But, if architecture is frozen music, the tune Mark's new church played was not an ancient traditional hymn, but a straightforward melody of practical service to a dying community. No fancy spires pushed up through the polluted skies. No ornate furniture with cozy cushions reposed in the auditorium. There was no vestry of comfortable carpet or expensive drapes to flatter the ego of the pastor. This church was to be a hospital for dying souls, not a repository of fine art. The hurts of Calcutta were real, and planting flowers over the sewers would not make the filth go away.

Not long after the church was finished, Mark visited a family whose wife and mother had come to know the Lord. He called on the father, who was a well-known and rather wealthy Hindu in Calcutta. The man worked for a large insurance concern in India and was proud of his ancient religion. He was furious that Mark would dare impose Christianity on his family.

Jumping out of his chair, he shook his fist in Mark's face and spat out, "Don't try to tell me your Jesus is the Son of God!"

"Sir, there will come a day," Mark replied, "when God will prove to you that indeed Jesus is the Son of God."

With that, Mark turned and walked out of the house.

A few mornings later Mark received an urgent phone call from this insurance man's wife.

"Oh, Pastor Buntain," she gasped, "something terrible has happened. Please meet us at the government hospital. It is urgent!"

Mark threw on his coat and raced to the hospital.

The family had three children, two girls and a boy. The girls were bright and pretty, and the Hindu father had sent them to North India to a private school. The younger of the two daughters, Suman, had failed her final examination in high school. To Indian young people this is a great disgrace.

The day the two girls came home, Suman did not tell her family about the test results. That night they all attended a party.

The following day was a holiday, so the girls' mother let them sleep late. Before long the older girl came down for breakfast, but the younger still slept. After some time the mother became worried about her daughter and sent her son to check on his sister.

When he turned back the sheets on her bed he screamed for his mother.

Suman's body was turning black. She had swallowed a lethal dosage of pills in an effort to kill herself. They could hardly tell if she was dead or alive.

The family rushed Suman to the hospital, and the mother called Mark to meet them there. By this time the father had shown up, wringing his hands in desperation. Mark entered the hospital room and watched the doctors scrambling to save her life. But it seemed certain she would die.

Mark saw God's plan unfolding. He walked up to the chief doctor and said, "Please sir, let me be alone with Suman for one moment." The doctor had given up on her, so he nodded and stepped back.

Mark looked down on the beautiful face of the dying girl. By now her eyes were sunken. She gasped for every breath in her unconscious state. As the Holy Spirit directed Mark's words, he turned to find the girl's father.

"Do you remember," Mark asked, "what I said to you just a few days ago? I told you there would come a day when God would prove to you that Jesus is indeed the Son of God."

"I remember," said the weeping father.

"Sir, will you believe Jesus is the Son of God if He heals your daughter?"

"Yes, pastor, I will believe. The doctors say she cannot live. If she does, I will know it was because of your Jesus."

Mark left the family at the hospital and returned that afternoon. Suman had been removed to a private room where they were waiting for her to die. Mark stood in the doorway of that hospital room and prayed, "O God, please heal Suman and show this family that Jesus is your Son."

Again Mark left the hospital and Suman's condition did not improve. Two hours later he returned. Several tangled tubes were attached to her body. Her father and mother, along with the president of the father's insurance firm, were keeping the deathwatch by her bed. In a few minutes Suman would die, unless a miracle occurred.

"As I stepped into the room," Mark remembers,

"I felt a mighty surge of God's Spirit. I walked over to the bed and spoke to the unconscious girl. 'Suman, in the name of Jesus Christ, come out of this unconsciousness.' A big tear rolled down her cheek. I knew God had touched her, because unconscious people do not cry."

Suman started to whimper and pull at the straps that tied her to the bed.

"Untie her," Mark ordered the nurse. "Jesus is healing Suman."

The nurse backed off. She had never seen anything like this. Finally, wide-eyed, she obeyed this strange white sahib.

Within moments Suman sat up, blinking and squinting, trying to focus her eyes.

Immediately the news shot through the hospital. Suman's doctors ran in. They were incredulous. Then after a moment, they made a grim prediction: "Your daughter is past her crisis, but we must warn you that her mind will be permanently damaged."

For the second time a surge of faith came over Mark.

"Sir, you told me if God would heal your daughter, you would confess Him as your Savior," Mark said to the father. "Do you still stand by that commitment?"

"I will, I will," the father said.

"Then I am going to believe God that, by this time tomorrow, your daughter will be absolutely well."

Mark turned and walked out of the room.

When he visited the family the next day, Suman was sitting up in bed combing her hair. She had a happy smile on her face—completely healed.

A little later, Suman was dismissed from the hospital and went back to school. There was absolutely no brain damage.

And the Hindu father, true to his word, confessed Jesus Christ as his personal Savior.

These impulses or impressions that Mark gets from God often seem mystical. However, they are the practical results of a life of prayer and obedience to the Spirit of God. One Sunday evening, one of the church ladies asked Mark to pray for her boss. He worked for Standard Oil of India and was desperately ill in one of the government hospitals. Mark agreed to remember him in prayer.

Later that week Mark felt impressed to visit a certain hospital. He did not know where the girl's boss was—or if he was even in that particular hospital. When he felt the impression, he didn't even know why he should stop by. But Mark went.

Standing in the doorway of one of the wards, Mark looked over the crowded cots. Halfway across the room stood a lady crying near an Indian man who lay gasping for breath in one of the beds. Mark walked over to her and introduced himself. He asked if he could pray for her husband. She agreed, without understanding all that Mark was doing. Anything that would help her husband was all right with her.

God touched the man, and slowly he recovered.

Later Mark learned this was the same man for whom the church girl had requested prayer. Several weeks later, this man and his whole family showed up at Mark's church. When the altar call was given, the whole family came forward, giving their hearts to God.

A few weeks after his conversion, this Standard Oil executive became hungry for the deeper things of God. Mark remembers that one night he came to the prayer room and announced he would not leave there until he received the pentecostal baptism. He took off his shoes, placed them beside him on the floor, and began to pray. Within minutes God honored the sincerity of the seeker, and he was filled with the Spirit. Later he left Standard Oil and became a preacher of the gospel, traveling all across Canada and the United States, sharing the love of Jesus Christ. Today he is still an international evangelist, preaching throughout Europe and Asia.

Trevor was another "brand from the burning" whom Mark rescued. Trevor had been a police officer during the 1947 riots that tore through Calcutta in the wake of independence. The carnage and death left him shell-shocked and addicted to alcohol. Trevor's family gave up on him, and now he lived on the streets.

One night someone invited Trevor to Mark's mission. He had been drinking heavily and, having nothing better to do, decided to go and see the show. He was trembling and weak—practically palsied, physically bankrupt from the effects of alcohol. Something in Mark's sermon got through his whiskey-soaked mind, and Trevor stumbled down to the altar. God saved him, and instantly his mind was sobered. The next night he was healed; his body was restored to wholeness.

Slowly Trevor was able to put his life back together. With Mark's help he got a job with British Airways as a security officer. The airline liked Trevor so much that they later transferred him to Toronto, Canada, where he still lives and shares the love of Jesus with the youth of that city.

Daily, Mark prowled the streets of Calcutta to save the dying. Not only was he reaching the Hindus and Moslems, but he was also snatching backslidden Christians from the lips of hell. One such young man was Danny Paul.

Danny had been raised in southern India. He was from a poor family and, as soon as he was old enough to work, came to Calcutta hoping to find a job.

Danny's family were Christians; in fact, Danny's uncle was in Mark's church. But when the young man went to Calcutta, the lure of the lights was too great for him. Before long he had lost himself in the night life of Calcutta. He worked during the day for Indian Airlines, but he didn't make much money and had little hope of a future. He earned enough to buy whiskey and make fast friends, though, and Danny accepted this lot in life. If he had no future, Danny was at least going to enjoy the present.

One night, after an exhausting day, Mark Buntain was preparing for bed. He was bone-tired and looked forward to slipping under the covers for a little rest. It was already long past his usual bedtime.

Just then, that familiar inner voice spoke to him. He knew he had to put on his clothes and go out into the night, although he had no idea where.

Mark dressed hastily and left Huldah. God, he explained, was sending him on a mission. She understood these night jaunts. Although she always worried about him, she had long ago learned that she too must listen when that inner voice spoke.

Driving north from his home, Mark came to Center Road. There he stopped. He prayed silently.

"Now, Lord, you brought me here for a purpose. Please let me know what it is."

Just then a car came cruising by, filled with five laughing and obviously drunk young men. Although he didn't recognize the teen-agers, Mark pulled out from the curb and swerved around the car, pulling it to the curb. When he peered inside, he saw Danny Paul sitting in the back seat.

"What are you doing here at this time of night?" the boy blurted out to Mark.

"That is not the question, Danny," Mark said. "The question is, what are you doing here? God has a call on your life, and you are going home with me."

The boy meekly obeyed. Later Danny recommitted his life to Christ and became one of Mark's deacons.

A few years later Mark received a phone call from Swiss Airlines, asking him to recommend an honest young man for a most responsible position. Mark recommended Danny, and the company immediately liked him. He rose to become a superintendent for Swiss Air in India. Later Danny and his family migrated to Canada, where he now works for the University of Toronto. He also preaches throughout Ontario about the Christ he loves.

Another strange encounter came some time later. It was a Sunday evening, and Mark was running late for the 6:30 service. Moving through the Calcutta traffic can be exasperating as you dodge the cows, children, ancient taxi cabs, and carts piled high with jute.

Just as Mark started to turn his car into the church compound, he felt an inner prompting to go in the opposite direction. After a momentary argument with the inner voice, Mark obeyed. The service would have to start without him.

He drove to McCloud Street and felt compelled to turn onto a small muddy lane. There was hardly room to get the small car through, but he squeezed in. Then he saw the man.

Lying in a gutter beside the tiny lane was a filthy, hopeless drunk. Immediately Mark knew this was his mission of mercy for the evening. He got out of the car and lifted the wretched drunk from the open sewer. Mud splashed on Mark's clothes, and the man threw up on him. Mark maneuvered the drunk into his car and took him to the church office.

Later, when he got the man sobered, he learned that his name was Fred, and he had been a truck driver for Shell Oil of India—a responsible and good-paying job. He became a hopeless alcoholic whose drinking habits caused his family to lose their home. They now lived in the squalor of a bustee.

Mark talked to Fred, and he gave his heart to God. Inexplicably, Mark believed God was going to do a remarkable work in his life.

A few days later Mark took Fred to his former employers and asked the supervisor if he would take the man back to work. The boss flatly refused. This was already the third time they had fired Fred. The final dismissal had come specifically because of his drunkenness—along with the fact that he had filed false vouchers with the company. Under no circumstances would they ever rehire him.

"Sir," Mark asked, "do you believe Jesus Christ can change a man?"

"Yes, I do," the boss replied sternly, "but we will still not take him back."

Mark insisted.

"I said, 'Sir, do you believe Jesus Christ can change a man?' "

Finally the supervisor had taken enough.

"Reverend, I'll take him back only if the president of the company tells me to," the boss told him. "If I did this on my own, I would have a rebellion on my hands. I have fired hundreds of men for drinking. Thousands are seeking jobs right now. I won't do anything unless the company president tells me to."

Mark asked the president's name and learned that one of the girls in his church served as the president's secretary. Mark made an appointment with the president, and soon found himself repeating the story of how he found Fred and what Jesus had done for him. As he ended the story, he said to the president, "Sir, do you believe Jesus Christ can change a man?"

"That has nothing to do with this," the president replied gruffly.

Mark quietly asked again, "Sir, do you really believe Jesus Christ can change a man?"

Again the president refused. Mark asked the piercing question again.

Finally the president broke down. He would give Fred one more chance.

That was all Fred needed. He became one of the company's finest drivers and a leader in Mark's church. Several years later Fred was promoted to security officer, and finally he joined Mark's staff. He still works for Mark today, faithfully serving the Lord he loves and the pastor who pulled him out of the gutter. Fred's family is reunited, and they all go to Mark's church.

Almost daily God leads the needy of Calcutta into the arms of a man who can lift them up with the love of Jesus.

13

The Compassionate Touch

Alcoholics have been cured, cripples healed, and shattered lives mended at Royd Street. But Mark and Huldah do not wait for people to come and visit the church; they go into the highways and hedges and compel them to come in.

One day Huldah visited one of the bustees in Calcutta, feeding and helping the poor. At one door, a young mother invited her in. She had seven children, and two of the little girls were so emaciated from hunger that they were too weak to get up off the floor. The father had become an alcoholic. What little money he made was spent on whiskey.

Huldah moved to help the struggling family. The girls were fed and clothed. They began coming to the church and gave their hearts to the Lord. Their father saw the difference in his family, and he too committed his heart to Christ.

Those little girls have now grown up. One, Joyce Druart, is Mark's secretary; the other teaches in his school.

Another staff member Mark has touched with his life is Denzil Wood. Denzil was born into an English family that had fallen on hard times. He and his family lived on the top floor of a shabby apartment in the heart of the city.

Denzil contracted tuberculosis as a boy. Mark visited the family frequently. Over thirty times Mark climbed the five flights of stairs to take a doctor to Denzil so he could get injections for the disease.

One night the family called Mark in a panic. Denzil was hemorrhaging. Mark rushed over and prayed fervently. That night, God touched the young teen-ager, and his health returned.

Three years later Denzil left Calcutta and took employment in England. There he slipped away from the Lord, although he was doing very well financially. But deep down, Denzil yearned for the things of God, and while attending a Youth for Christ meeting in London, he rededicated his heart to the Lord.

When Youth for Christ sponsored a congress of prayer in Calcutta, Denzil returned to his hometown to attend. What he saw in the city of his birth haunted him. When he returned to England, God continued to stir his heart. One night Denzil called Mark and asked if he could come to Calcutta and help with the work. Mark was delighted; Denzil became an answer to Mark's prayer. Today Denzil works with the youth of the church and does a great deal of administrative work for Mark.

Royd Street continued to be a hospital for sick souls. One night as Mark was in the prayer room, a disheveled youth staggered into the church. He sought out the pastor and said, "I must have help. I am a Hindu and an alcoholic. I have a job with the airlines, but they are about to fire me because of my drinking. I've tried everything, but I can't quit. My gods can't help me. You are my last hope."

"Sir, will you fall on your knees right now," Mark said, "and claim Jesus Christ as your personal Savior? He will help you."

In his desperation, the young drunk fell to his knees and began crying out, "Jesus, please help me!" He was so loud that he could be heard in the street.

The young man was instantly saved and sobered. Today he too is a part of Mark's church.

Late one night one of Mark's deacons rapped on his door.

"Pastor, we have an urgent problem. Near our house there is a young man who has lost his mind. Will you come and help us?"

Mark dressed and followed his deacon into the night. When they arrived at the home, Mark learned the youth was deeply involved in the drug culture of

Calcutta. The drugs had thrown him into wild rages, and he had beaten his wife and child mercilessly. They had left him. The youth had often threatened his own mother's life, and just the night before he had been beaten into unconsciousness by a roving gang during one of his drug stupors. They had dumped him at his mother's door, and now he was coming out of his haze, raging like a wild animal.

When Mark walked into the bedroom, the drug-dazed man was doubled over on the bed, writhing in agony, seething with fury. The pastor knew instinctively that demonic powers had overtaken the young man. Taking spiritual authority, Mark prayed with fervor and commanded the unclean spirits to leave the young man. The boy immediately stopped writhing and dropped off into a calm sleep. The boy's mother had never seen anything like this. Mark turned to her.

"Ma'am, your son is in this terrible condition," he told her, "because he has left Jesus out of his life. Perhaps you too have left Him out of your life. I will wait here, and I want you to go into your bedroom, fall on your knees, and accept Jesus Christ as your Lord and Savior."

She obeyed, and another new soul was born that night into the kingdom.

By this time the police had arrived. They were going to take the youth to an asylum, but Mark intervened. The boy was sleeping.

After a while the young man awoke and saw Mark

standing by his bed. He began to cry uncontrollably. Soon Mark had led him to a knowledge of Jesus Christ.

Later in the day, Mark felt impressed to return to the little house. When he did, he found the boy suffering great pain from the beating he had received.

"Tom, Jesus laid hands on the sick," Mark told him, "and they recovered. Do you believe He can heal you?"

The new convert, fresh in his faith, responded enthusiastically, "Yes!"

Mark prayed and left. As Mark was getting in his car, the youth shouted after him.

"Wait for me, pastor! The pain is gone!"

During the next few days, Mark was able to counsel with the young man and his estranged wife. They began coming to church on Royd Street. Mark always thrilled to see them sitting there, as newlyweds would, hand in hand, or walking out of the church with arms tenderly intertwined.

But perhaps among the thousands of stories Mark could tell about remarkable redemption, the case of Michael and Andree best explains how God uses this missionary to rescue souls at the brink of hell.

Andree was born into an affluent family. She was beautiful even as a baby, and grew up to become "Miss Calcutta." As a child she had met Mark's daughter, Bonnie. The two girls were fond of each other, and Andree spent many hours in the Buntain home.

But Andree's family were not Christians. Her mother was an entertainer, singing in a night club owned by the family.

After becoming "Miss Calcutta," Andree sought the bright lights and thrills of the entertainment world. India has one of the largest movie industries in the world, with Bombay being the Eastern equivalent of Hollywood. Andree wanted to become a movie actress, and there was great expectation she would make it.

About this time she met a young man who swept her off her feet, and within a few weeks they had been married in a civil ceremony. But the marriage was strained from the start. Each wanted plenty from the other, but neither wanted to give very much. In addition, Andree had her heart set on becoming a famous movie actress.

Before long, the pair separated in a bitter battle. Although they loved each other, their own selfishnesses kept them from working through their problems. It was during this separation that Andree attended a Sunday night service on Royd Street. She had never come before, even though she knew the Buntains from her childhood.

Something happened to Mark when he saw Andree walk into the service. He knew nothing of her circumstances, but the Holy Spirit placed a deep burden on his heart at that moment. After the service he spoke to her for a moment, and she told him about the broken marriage. Mark pleaded with her to accept Christ, but Andree had no time for God. She wanted a career, money, fame. It was too bad about her marriage, she said, but she would get over it.

Mark could not get Andree and Michael out of his mind. They haunted him—until eventually some of the staff members became irritated by Mark's constant focus on them.

One night Mark retired early to get some much-needed rest. By 11:20 P.M. he had awakened, weeping. He prayed all night for Andree and Michael, until finally falling to sleep at six in the morning. When he left for his office he was still praying, "Jesus, I must see Michael today. I don't know where he is, but please let me talk with him."

It was true Mark had no idea where to meet the young man who had married Andree. But at 9:30 that morning, while Mark was in his office, there was a sharp rap at the door. It was Michael. He slumped into one of Mark's chairs and sighed, "Sir, I want to change my life."

That morning, Mark led Michael to the Lord. Tears of joy washed down his face, and there was a new light on the boy's face.

Mark, however, knew the battle was just beginning. Andree wanted no part of the marriage. She was not interested in Christ. Her heart was set on a movie career.

For four weeks the battle for Andree's soul raged.

Michael was willing to do what he could to put the marriage back together, but nothing he could say would help.

Mark became a man obsessed. He prayed for hours on end for Andree. Staff members began to complain because they could not get him to make urgent decisions about the mission work. His heart and mind were totally occupied with this burden. He wrote slips of paper and handed them to every Christian he met—"Pray for Andree."

One day during the four-week battle, he felt he had to see Andree and talk with her. She was working as a model, and he didn't know where to find her. Mark got in his car and headed toward the part of the city where clothing is sold. He saw Andree getting out of a car, but she had a photographer with her and she did not want to talk.

Mark decided to fast. He could no longer see her; she was avoiding the persistent preacher. All he could do was fast and pray. He resolved not to touch water or food until Andree was saved.

One day the Calcutta weather turned blisteringly hot. Mark had promised to preach at the Tilagarth Crusade, fifteen miles from Calcutta. He could not get out of the engagement, although by now he was weak from thirst and hunger and his skin was wrinkling.

Driving through the rutted roads jammed with lorries, buses, cars, oxen carts, and playing children, Mark hardly noticed the deep holes and crowded highway. He was pleading in prayer for Andree's soul.

Mark arrived at the tent where the meeting would take place. During the song service and testimonies, Mark's mind was on Andree.

"Jesus, save Andree," he kept whispering.

Then he stepped to the pulpit and opened his Bible; his tongue was so swollen he could hardly speak. He felt a wave of dizziness. But the Holy Spirit is a quickening Spirit, and Mark preached with power in spite of his personal weakness.

After the service Mark walked to his car to drive back to Calcutta. One of the pastors brought him a drink of delicious, fresh coconut milk.

"You must take this, Pastor Buntain," he insisted.

"No, I cannot," Mark replied.

They kept pressing Mark until finally he told them about the fast. He spoke through tears.

"Please, dear ones, please pray for Andree."

At night Mark could hardly sleep because of the heavy prayer burden.

Finally one morning, Andree showed up at Mark's office. She had brought Michael with her. She was ready to give her heart to the Lord and try again with her marriage.

It was a joyous morning for Mark. The three prayed together, and Andree was gloriously saved.

Later that week, Mark baptized both Michael and Andree in water. He also persuaded them to have a religious wedding ceremony, since they had only repeated their vows in front of a secular official.

Mark, Andree, and Michael prepared the wedding. It was a beautiful church ceremony, with many tears. Several of Andree's friends turned to Christ through this witness.

When the wedding was over, Mark handed a hotel key to Michael. The missionary had rented a room in Calcutta's finest hotel for Michael and Andree. He told them to spend their honeymoon there. When they arrived at the hotel they found that Mark had sent flowers.

Mark sent Michael and Andree to work with the missionary organization, "Youth With A Mission," in Hawaii. There the young couple were deeply touched by the power of God, and things began to happen in their lives to draw them nearer to Christ—and to each other.

Mark does move through the streets of Calcutta, looking for the wounded and needy of that city. He mends crippled souls and touches lonely lives with the love of his Lord. He is a man moved by compassion.

But not everyone in Calcutta sees him that way.

14

A Bitter Pill

Raw and ugly prejudice forced Mark to start his school on Royd Street. Sadly, it was not prejudice from the Hindus or Moslems that created the trouble, but from the small Christian community. But "Sweet are the uses of adversity," Shakespeare noted centuries ago, "Which like the toad, ugly and venomous, Wears yet a precious jewel in his head; And this our life, exempt from the public haunt, Finds tongues in trees, books in the running brooks, Sermons in stones, and good in everything."

As the mission on Royd Street started to grow, the two previous bastions of the Christian faith in Calcutta looked with suspicion on the strange little work in the heart of the city. For several centuries the Anglican and Roman Catholic churches had been the Christian influence in Calcutta, and they resented this "invader" that had entered their territory.

The "strange things going on down there" also unsettled them. Perhaps changed lives justified what was happening, but they were nonetheless skeptical of all-night prayer meetings, people speaking in tongues, and emotional services so full of crying. Even the fast growth of the mission, they reasoned, must indicate something was wrong somewhere.

The churches were not in danger of competition. In a city of nine million souls, even after centuries of Christian influence, only about 10 percent of Calcutta's population claimed Christianity. There have certainly always been plenty of souls to go around. If all the churches of Calcutta worked in perfect harmony, the task of reaching the lonely and lost would still be overwhelming.

But even the very good can sometimes act and react very badly. Mark was to find this out. And, this was most profound in the area of education.

When India's independence was declared and freedom came on that spectacular midnight of August 15, 1947, everything that reminded the new country of their former rulers was despised. The highly organized educational system set up by the British was one of the first things to go. Unwisely, the new Indian government put all of their educational funds and emphases in and on the university systems. They thought little about the future, and almost immediately the primary school system fell into disrepair. Schools were closed, and primary education was left to various missions that dotted the city.

Naturally, the Anglicans and Roman Catholics had the best facilities and budgets. These schools soon became the only schools. To this day only about 40 percent of the Calcutta children ever get to see the inside of a classroom.

As revival swept Royd Street, the established churches felt they must put a stop to Mark's mission. A perfect way to handle this was pressure through the church-controlled educational system. During those days, Mark sent buses through the city to pick up children for Sunday school. The children loved to ride the buses, and they came by the hundreds. Soon Catholic nuns—armed with notebooks and pencils—were standing at the stops where the children boarded Mark's buses. They recorded the name of each child riding Mark's bus, and on Monday morning each child got a notice of expulsion from school.

One Monday morning, Mark arrived at the church to find 250 children with their parents waiting for him. The children had all been expelled from their schools and the parents wanted to know what Mark could do about it—particularly since their commitment to his ministry had created the problem.

Frankly, Mark did not know what to do. He had no influence with the established churches, and his budget was already so strained he could not start a school of his own. But he had known from the start that a school was desperately needed.

"When we came to Calcutta," Mark recalled later, "we learned 60 percent of all children under age twelve were not in any school."

Mark did the only thing he knew how to do—he prayed.

The problem was not readily solved.

When the Buntains had finished their sixth year in Calcutta, it was time for them to return to America and raise funds for the next term. Mark decided that while he was home he would also seek permission from the Foreign Missions Board to start a school in Calcutta.

This would be no easy job. The Assemblies of God have traditionally preferred to invest their missionary dollars in churches and Bible schools, not educational systems, hospitals, or orphanages. Traditionally, the denomination has stayed away from social concern, to concentrate instead on the spiritual problems facing mankind.

Men with greater minds than Mark's had argued the point, but no one had succeeded in getting the Assemblies involved in a school. Knowing the battle ahead, Mark asked his Calcutta people to pray. And then he took his family home to America for a much-needed rest.

For five days Mark met and argued with the board about his need for a school. They listened. They understood, but still they had to think of the implications for the rest of the world, not just Calcutta. After all, the denomination was world-wide—and if they set a precedent, would they lose their distinguishing and effective missionary emphasis? It was a difficult time for both Mark and the dedicated men who served on the Foreign Missions Board.

Finally on the fifth day, the question was set to be resolved. Mark made an impassioned plea, calling attention to the heartbreak of the Calcutta parents who had to choose between serving Christ in the Royd Street church or seeing their children get through school. He reminded the men that the decision these parents made was not easy, since jobs were virtually impossible to get in Calcutta without a good education. And, only if their children worked could the family have security, since India had no welfare system to care for its down-and-outers.

Mark sat down. After a moment the chairman spoke.

"Mark, I'm sorry. We believe everything you say. We understand your need, but we cannot help you. We can't give you one dollar. If you insist on starting a school, you will do it totally on your own."

"But I've never been on my own," Mark replied quickly. "God has always been with me. I'm not asking for the money, I'm asking for permission."

Many missionaries have found that pardon is easier than permission, so they move ahead with their projects and later notify the missions board. But Mark would have none of that. He wanted to keep things right and operate with the utmost integrity. He knew it was the only way God would bless his work.

Suddenly another board member jumped up and said, "I object to giving Mark permission. Why should he be allowed to raise money from our churches for a school, when we have such a desperate need for a Bengali church in Calcutta?"

In a flash of inspiration Mark jumped in.

"Sirs, if you will give me permission to build my school," he told the board, "I will raise the money for the Bengali church."

The tide turned and the mission board gave permission. They allocated no funds for Mark's school. He was indeed on his own. However, he could tell churches about the need—and if they wanted to help, that was their business.

Mark crisscrossed the United States. It was an exhausting year of travel, living in different motel rooms every night. He not only had to visit the churches which already sponsored him so he could share what had happened with their investment—but he had to seek out new churches for support.

Month after month he lugged his heavy projectors and slides around America and Canada, trying to stir up a fire of concern for people half a world away.

By the end of the year, Mark had raised the money, but the physical cost was also great. The endless weeks of exertion took a devastating physical toll on him, and, although he didn't know it then, his course had been set for a physical and emotional breakdown in the days ahead. Soon he would be plunged into a labyrinth of confusion—a pit so deep that he would even wonder if God cared. At this moment, though, he was happy.

Armed with commitments to the Bengali church and the school, Mark, Huldah, and Bonnie headed back to Calcutta to start their new work. From the beginning they had hundreds of children and a growing staff. The quality of the school soon grew in reputation—so that parents who had once had their children in the Anglican and Catholic schools wanted to transfer them to Mark's system. He would teach hundreds of Hindu and Moslem children, making a deep impact on Calcutta.

But because of the harsh opposition from the Catholics and Anglicans, Mark permitted bitterness to slip slowly into his heart. He didn't notice it at first, but at times his sermons would be laced with invectives against the oppression of the Roman church and the Anglican diocese. Some of the Anglo-Indians in his congregation had converted from the Roman Catholic church, and they often told him stories of oppression. This made him more angry. At times Mark had to preach funerals for the poor Roman Catholics who could not afford the ten-rupee funeral fee imposed by the church.

But God would not allow that bitterness to take root permanently in Mark's heart. Through several divine appointments God helped him work through his frustration. Mark remembers walking down the streets of Calcutta one day when the city's most prestigious Anglican priest stopped him and scathingly rebuked him.

"You and your born-again experience," the priest sneered. "Who do you think you are? Why don't you get out of here and leave us alone?"

Years later Mark would have the joy of seeing this same priest make a total turnaround and lead a public prayer of gratefulness and blessing for the Royd Street work. God, through the years, began healing the hurts between those who named the name of Christ—though often they differed in doctrine and direction.

Without question, the greatest bitterness Mark felt was against the Roman Catholic church. He had seen school leaders abusing the poor of Calcutta. He felt the priests were often unfeeling, willing to sacrifice people for the sake of the church. The bitterness built slowly through the years, until a time when Mark would cross to the other side of the street whenever a Roman Catholic priest or nun would walk toward him. He felt these people were traitors to the cross of Christ.

While he was still in Calcutta he read periodicals

about a great outpouring of God's Spirit at Notre Dame, the Catholic school. He heard about stirrings within the Catholic church, of people there who were turning on to Jesus.

At first Mark dismissed all this. His anger would not let him believe that anyone in the Catholic system could have experiences like those being reported. Certainly people were being touched by the Spirit of God, Mark reasoned, but he had no use for them if they didn't come out of the Catholic church and get into a fundamental circle. With this attitude Mark returned home on furlough.

Each year the Assemblies of God sponsors a School of Missions for all the missionaries home on furlough. Mark attended, and the speakers for that particular session were ministers who had been deeply involved in the Notre Dame outpouring. They talked about how God was pouring out His Spirit on *all* denominations.

"I sat in my seat as hard as stone," Mark recalls. "I refused to bend. I could understand how that maybe, just maybe, such a thing could happen in America; but it would *never* happen in India."

After the sermon, the missionaries were shown a documentary film of the Notre Dame revival. Mark saw 4,000 priests and nuns standing in a great auditorium with hands raised, praising God. They sang "How Great Thou Art," and many were even speaking in tongues.

Then the film recorded a young priest giving a

beautiful message of prophecy concerning the second coming of Christ. Tears started to roll down Mark's face, but still he could not accept it. He stood up and hurried out of the service.

Later Mark was walking across the campus of the School of Missions. An outdoor theater had been set up, and they were showing the Notre Dame film again. Mark refused to turn his head and watch it.

After the school closed, Mark traveled to California for missionary meetings. He was slated to speak the next Sunday at Sunnyvale, near San Francisco. After he settled into his motel room, Mark went over to the church to ask the pastor if he could borrow a tape recorder to get some dictation done.

"Oh, Mark, we have a meeting starting in a few minutes," the pastor said. "We have a Roman Catholic priest speaking. Would you please stay and hear him?"

In his heart Mark wanted to stay, but his head told him no. He made an excuse and started his car. Then that old inner voice spoke again; Mark heard it in the deep recesses of his heart.

There is something here I want you to learn.

Mark turned off the engine and went back inside.

Mark captures that moment in thoughtful retrospect.

"For the first time in my life, I heard a Catholic priest teach on the baptism of the Holy Spirit. I heard several other Catholics give testimonies of how Jesus had come into their hearts, and they too had been filled with the Spirit.

"God was dealing with me. After the service I went up to the priest and put my arms around him. I told him of my bitterness and anger. God began to heal my bitter heart."

During that meeting God spoke to Mark about a task he had to perform when he returned to Calcutta. Mark knew that when he returned he would have to go to the Roman Catholic bishop of Calcutta and ask forgiveness for all the bitterness he had harbored toward the Catholics for years. It was a heavy assignment that would mean swallowing his pride and groveling before those who had given Mark and his people so many problems.

But the voice was unmistakable. Regardless of how bitter the pill is God asks us to swallow, He always seems to know how to give a little sugar to help the medicine go down. This is what happened to Mark.

Just before he returned to Calcutta, Mark had one last meeting in Chicago. He visited the home of Bud and Candy Zimmerman. Bud is a psychologist and son of the general superintendent of the Assemblies of God. There Mark met another Catholic priest.

They shook hands and Mark told him, "I can't call you 'father,' but I will call you 'brother.'"

The priest replied, "Why don't you just call me 'Bill,' and I will call you 'Mark.'"

Mark and the priest sat down over coffee. Mark

was still struggling with his skepticism, although he could no longer question the divine moving of God. He started asking Bill questions to test his theology.

Finally the priest smiled, "Mark, I don't want to hurt your feelings," he said, "but I probably know more theology than you have ever learned. I am a graduate of seven seminaries. If you want to discuss theology, I can discuss it from any level you want.

"But, Mark, even though I have been a priest for many years and have studied from the age of fourteen, it was only three years ago that I came to know the Lord Jesus as my personal Savior. He has come into my heart. He has filled me with His precious Holy Spirit and changed my life. And that's all I want to talk about."

Their bond of fellowship was welded that night. Mark told the priest about his heavy assignment back in Calcutta—apologizing to the bishop of Calcutta and explaining that he now understood how all Christians—including himself—could at times display pettiness and anger. Mark confessed all the bitterness and anger he had carried through the years.

When he finished, the priest said, "Mark, if you will let me, I will go back to Calcutta with you. I will pay all my own expenses, and I promise not to do anything that will hurt you. I'll go with you to the bishop, if you want."

The unlikely pair got off the plane in Calcutta to meet a surprised congregation. The church immediately fell in love with Bill, and all the deep scars started to heal from the hurts of years gone by. Within a few days an appointment was made with Calcutta's Roman Catholic bishop, and Mark and Bill kept it.

The meeting began somewhat tensely, with the bishop demanding to see Bill's credentials for being there. Then he mellowed.

"Sir, all these years I have had bitterness toward you and your church," Mark began. "But back in America, God spoke to my heart, and I know I have been wrong.

"I have come to ask you to forgive me. There may be things we will never agree on, but I promise my attitude will never again be what it was. Will you forgive me?"

The old bishop was visibly moved. He told Mark he was forgiven, and then he leaned forward in his chair for Mark and Bill to tell him more about this "new blessing."

"I have studied for the priesthood since I was a boy," Bill explained, "but never had a personal relationship with God until three years ago. It changed my life, and the baptism of the Holy Spirit gave me such a hunger for God that I have fallen deeply in love with His Word. Once I had trouble getting people to hear my sermons. Now my problem is I have more people than I have messages."

Before Mark and Bill left the bishop's office, they

all prayed together. The bishop said, "Bill, I am directing my entire diocese to open their pulpits for you to preach." For the next few weeks Bill preached to masses in the Calcutta Catholic churches and Mark's Sunday evening services.

Since then, that bishop has become a cardinal. Today Catholic churches in Calcutta are slowly beginning to experience this "new blessing." Their attitudes have thawed toward outsiders, just as Mark's did toward them. In Calcutta there is now one Catholic Bengali church that is charismatic. There is a Catholic pentecostal group in Bangalore, and some of the priests have been drawn close to the Spirit. One of their bishops has now been filled with the Spirit. Bombay is experiencing the same move in its Roman Catholic churches. Healing of torn and bleeding churches is taking place.

God had taught Mark that it is easy to judge people by their lowest, rather than their highest, expressions. This prompted Mark to ask the Father to forgive him—and to readjust his eyesight, so that he could see the best in people and organizations.

Not long ago, the vicar of Calcutta's most prestigious Anglican church called on Mark at the church office. He asked Mark to pray with him to accept Christ and be filled with the Holy Spirit. The young vicar now has a deep and meaningful ministry that is touching lives throughout Calcutta.

"God has given my dear brother a precious ministry of prayer, healing, and compassion," Mark reports. "He is a beautiful brother. Our Lord is so faithful."

15

Breakdown

Dietrich Bonhoeffer, martyred in Nazi Germany by Hitler's mindless minions, once said, "When Christ calls a man, He bids him come and die."

Mark was indeed giving his life for the needs and the needy of Calcutta. And even though he had always been in excellent health, the wear and tear of his schedule, the heavy demands on his time, and the growing budget of his work made the burden almost unbearable.

A sensitive man who easily picks up nonverbal cues, Mark is deeply affected by the sorrow about him. He cannot turn off the grieving, but carries the burdens of his people wherever he goes. While his great compassion is without doubt his greatest virtue, it can also have a devastating effect on his nervous system.

One of the deepest hurts he suffered came when a ball of fire exploded in Calcutta's airport in the middle of the dark night.

Missionaries know a companionship that runs deep. Loyalty and love grow strong between strangers in a foreign land. The missionaries to India were no exception. At conferences and retreats, friendships were renewed and deepened.

The Dillinghams were close friends of the Buntains. They had five growing and lively children. The youngest, Suzanne, was a close chum of Bonnie Buntain. The girls had played together often, and their affection for each other was well known.

Toward the end of one of their furloughs, the Dillinghams were forced to send young Suzanne back to India ahead of them so she could start school. The boarding school she was to attend was very strict about these matters, and there was no other way. They would join her in a few weeks.

Her schedule called for Suzanne to fly into New Delhi and wait at the airport alone until she could catch transportation to her school. International flights arrived in the early hours of the morning in New Delhi, since the heat there is so intense it often disturbs engine efficiency.

Learning that Suzanne would have to face it alone in New Delhi, Mark cabled the Dillinghams and suggested they send her to Calcutta. He would meet her and drive her on up to the school. This would assure the missionary family of their daughter's safety.

Bonnie wanted to go with her dad to pick up her friend, although the plane wouldn't arrive until shortly after 1:00 A.M. Mark agreed. And knowing Suzanne would be tired, Huldah prepared a fresh bed, clean clothing, and a warm snack for her.

Then Mark and Bonnie headed for the airport.

But Mark began to worry. A tropical storm was brewing, and something just did not feel right. He said nothing to his happy daughter, but he was distinctly uneasy.

When they arrived at the Pan Am ticket counter the rain had begun. Mark worried out loud to the attendant.

"Do you think they will try to land in weather like this?"

"Oh, don't worry," the man replied. "Those big 707s can come down in anything."

Mark wandered through the waiting area, looking nervously toward the runway. He paced restlessly back and forth, waiting.

Suddenly he saw a huge ball of fire light the skies, far from where the plane was supposed to land. He ran to the ticket counter.

"What has happened?" he demanded.

"It could not have been the Pan Am flight," the agent said, "since it is still in the air."

But Mark knew something terrible had

happened.

He deposited Bonnie with the agents and joined the screaming fire trucks and ambulances on the other side of the field.

The Pan Am flight had fallen far short of the runway and smashed into a grove of banana trees.

Passengers were jumping from the flaming wreck with their clothing afire. They screamed in pain and staggered through the blackness of the tropical night and the slashing rain. The injured looked like escapees from hell, with bloody faces and torn limbs.

Mark searched desperately for Suzanne but could not find her anywhere. Stretchers were carried into the terminal by the dozens. Mark searched each one for his little friend. Suzanne was not among the seventy wounded passengers.

Finally a doctor arrived and started helping Mark with the injured passengers.

"Were any left on the burning plane?" Mark asked anxiously.

"No, sir," he was told. "All got off, and though they are injured, all are alive. Perhaps an ambulance took your girl to the hospital near the airport."

Mark jumped into his car and raced the fifteen miles to Woodlands Nursing Home. There he found the battered and bleeding crew and asked if they remembered Suzanne. Yes, they remembered her, and they were sure she made it off.

But she was not at Woodlands.

Then the phone rang. It was for Mark. He was to

come back to the airport immediately. He knew it
was disaster.

Mark raced back to the airport, praying all the
fifteen miles. When he arrived, he was given the
news. At first they had thought all the passengers
were off. But apparently the tail section of the plane
had broken away. In that section were six people, all
burned to death.

Suzanne was one of them.

The American Consul asked Mark to serve as
official chaplain and help with the dead and dying.
For the rest of the day he went mechanically through
his work, saying to himself over and over, "If only I
had not asked Suzanne's parents to send her through
Calcutta."

Mark knew Suzanne was in heaven, but he had to
call America and break the news to the Dillinghams.
Their youngest daughter had been killed.

For weeks afterward, Mark fretted about his
responsibility in the crash. He knew in his heart that
everything was in the hands of God, but still he
could not wrench himself free from the grief he felt
he had caused.

A few days after the disaster, the Dillinghams flew
into Calcutta's airport. Mark was there to greet
them. When they walked off the plane, the customs
officials and ticket agents snapped to attention and
stood in reverence. Tears flowed as Mark embraced
the Dillinghams.

"I was so proud of those precious parents," he

says, "who still loved Jesus enough to come back to India after having given their precious daughter."

The Dillinghams continued to labor on the foreign field until they retired some years later. Suzanne is buried in Calcutta. The youth chapel of Mark's church is known as Suzanne Dillingham Hall.

So many hundreds had come to know the Lord—there were fantastic stories of changed lives—and Mark gloried in these. But there were also bitter disappointments, as many would take a hesitating step toward the kingdom and then back off when the tempter came up against them. Mark worried about these. He longed for every Indian to know the Lord. It was such a desperate burden to bear.

India also presented a special problem to its missionaries. Because of the massive population and limited space there is virtually no place a person can go to get away from people. Even when the Buntains would go on a family picnic, hungry children gathered around—even in the remotest area, hoping to eat leftovers from the missionaries' food basket.

In America, when pressures become intense, it is easy to rent a motel room or go to a cabin on a lake. There are no such facilities in India. Consequently, Mark could never escape the reality of his bleeding world.

When our team was in India, Mark took us on a picnic and we saw firsthand why he could never get away. We went into a remote area near the Bangladesh border and spread out our food. Within minutes, black-eyed children in ragged clothes gathered timidly about us.

A mangy dog waited nearby to grab any morsel of food we left. Even a couple of sacred Indian cows interrupted our meal. Our team had difficulty eating because of the hungry eyes watching us. We purposely left food, giving it to the hungry children.

Then there were the hungry, starving children of Calcutta. Famine swept Bengal, and the United Nations sent investigating teams to talk about the problems. Mark attended the meetings, and it seemed as though all they would do was talk. Mark knew the children who were dying—while argument went on about how to feed them.

Finally, in frustration, he told the United Nations representative, "Just give me the wheat; I will feed the children."

And with that, Mark Buntain started the first and most effective feeding kitchen in Calcutta. The United Nations made it possible for him to buy wheat and purchase milk from New Zealand, Canada, and Australia. He hired Indians to cook. And the starving children finally began getting food.

But there was so much to do and so little time. Mark's nerves were frayed.

Then, just a few months before their furlough, Huldah discovered she was pregnant.

The Buntains were overjoyed, yet apprehensive.

Mark and Huldah had a beautiful daughter, and they had longed for a son. But Calcutta was not the place they wanted to be when the baby was born. However, if nothing happened, they would be safely in the United States by the time Huldah was due to deliver.

In this state of exhaustion and tension, the Buntains left for America, to rest and to raise support for their work.

Huldah got sick on the way home. When they arrived, she was put in a hospital in California. Mark learned that a Calcutta doctor had accidentally poisoned her system by administering an improper medication.

Five doctors worked over Huldah for seventeen hours, trying to save her life. As the doctors fought for Huldah, Mark paced the floors of the Los Angeles hospital.

Mark was also in pain. He was suffering from a hernia so painful that he had been forced to sit down while preaching over the past few weeks in Calcutta. Within a few days it would demand surgery.

Late that night, the chief doctor left Huldah's side and went to Mark.

"I think we will be able to save your wife," the doctor said, "but the baby is dead."

Mark stood in the hall, grief-stricken. Happy new parents had been coming in all day to see their new babies. But there would be no son for Mark. If Huldah lived, the doctor said she would never again be able to bear children.

Mark turned and walked outside, tears drenching his face. He looked up into the night sky and saw a plane soaring overhead.

The inner voice spoke: *Mark, doesn't that plane have a pilot? I am the pilot of your life. Trust me.*

Mark thanked God for this comfort and went back inside to wait. At 10:30 they let Mark see his wife. She would be all right.

Oddly enough, furloughs drain missionaries—physically, mentally, emotionally, and spiritually. Mark had already fought his battle with the missions board for the new school, and now he had to raise the money for both the Bengali church and the Calcutta academy. He and Huldah were both exhausted when they started back to Calcutta. Huldah was still recuperating from her ordeal. Mark was to meet her in San Francisco, and together they would fly with Bonnie to Calcutta.

Mark arrived in San Francisco first. He was terribly tense and did not understand why. He had several hours to wait before Huldah and Bonnie arrived, and Mark knew he had to find somewhere to pray. Everything that had been nailed down seemed to be coming loose.

He couldn't pray at the airport; there had to be a church somewhere. Mark hailed a taxi and told the driver to take him to the only church he knew in San Francisco. Mark's heart was heavy, and he could not understand what was going on inside.

Winding through the city streets, the cabbie found Glad Tidings Church and deposited Mark at the door. Mark felt desperate. He needed someone to pray with him. He searched the building. There was no one there.

Great tears filled his eyes, and he fell at the altar to pray. But something was wrong. He could feel no comfort. The strangeness was still there. Something was going haywire.

Perhaps if Mark had recognized the symptoms, he would have stayed in the United States a few more months and rested. But there was so much to do. God would just have to take care of him. He had to go back to Calcutta.

Within a few days Mark was back at his desk, wrestling with the problems of the new school and the multitude of things that had to be done now that he was home.

"I was sitting at my desk," he remembers, "and suddenly I felt like a pile of bricks collapsed inside me. Tears began to run down my face. I couldn't stop them. I had to go home. I hailed a rickshaw and told the puller to get me home quickly. I went inside, sat at the table, and all I could do was cry."

Mark now knew he was having a breakdown. He knew he had to get to the mission home up in the mountains and try to rest. There was a hospital there, and he prayed he would be able to pull himself back together before it was too late.

Mark entered the missions hospital, but he got no

better. He could not sleep, although the doctors gave him massive doses of sleeping medicine. He kept his light on twenty-four hours a day. His emotions were shattered.

A kind doctor brought in a phonograph, and Mark listened by the hour to the singing of George Beverly Shea. It seemed to be the only thing that gave him rest.

The weeks passed. Every weekend Huldah and Bonnie would make the long trip to the mountains to see Mark. The car could take them only so far; they had to walk the rest of the way. But they faithfully came and tenderly nudged their broken loved one toward health.

Mark remembers the hour the crisis came. Unable to sleep for days, he finally got up from the hospital bed and put his clothes on. He told the nurses he was going for a walk. It was all over for Mark. He had reached the bottom. He felt there was no hope.

He walked to the little cottage where Huldah and Bonnie were staying. He went inside.

"Huldah, God has forsaken me," he said to his wife. "There is no hope for me. Why don't you and Bonnie go back to America and leave me to die? I am a forsaken man."

Just at that moment an elderly missionary rapped on the door. When Huldah let him in, he turned and said to Mark, "Come with me for a walk."

"No, brother," Mark said sadly, "I have walked

every path in these mountains, and I can't get better. Just leave me alone and forget about me."

"Please, Mark," the missionary said gently.

Mark reluctantly followed his friend along the small mountain path.

"Mark, I'm on my way to a Christian and Missionary Alliance pastor's home to pick up some Bibles," the missionary said. "Will you go with me?"

Mark did not want to meet anyone. He was shattered, and any strain felt overwhelming. But he was so numb that he kept on following his friend along the path.

When they arrived at the pastor's home, the host looked squarely at Mark.

"Mark," he said gently, "I walked your road one day."

The words stunned Mark.

"Those were the most precious words I have ever heard," Mark says today. "Was there hope? If God helped this dear brother back, could He not help me?"

"Mark, for two years I was much worse than you are now," the pastor told him. "In the deepest moment of my depression, God sent along a Christian doctor who simply told me, 'Remember, God loves you.' Those words were the turning point. I had said them to others so many times, but it was as if this was the first time I had ever heard them. From that moment I began to recover."

What had happened to that pastor happened in

that very moment to Mark. A tiny spark of hope finally flickered in his heart.

"In that moment," he says, "a wealth of wonderfulness swept over me. Inside I knew I was being healed. Immediately I wanted something to eat. This was unusual, because for weeks I had had no appetite."

When the two missionaries left the pastor's home, something deep had happened to Mark. He smiled for the first time. When he got to Huldah's cabin, he ran in and threw his arms around her.

"Jesus has touched me," he told her.

Within a few days Mark had recuperated greatly. He was sleeping now. He was eating well. His spirit of heaviness had been exchanged for the garment of praise. In just a few short weeks he returned to Calcutta—weak, but gaining strength every day.

The doctor had given medication to Mark as he left the hospital. On the train ride back to Calcutta, Mark went into the rest room, closed the door, and lifted his hands.

"I'm going back in the strength of your name," he told the Lord. "Please help me."

And he flushed the pills away.

When Mark arrived back in Calcutta, Tommy Barnett had come to Royd Street for an evangelistic crusade. At the end of the service, Mark asked the young preacher to pray for him for the complete healing of his emotions. At that moment, Jesus touched Mark and wiped the tears from his eyes.

God had taught him to rest more on the Lord than on his own strength. The agony of that experience has made Mark much wiser and more effective.

Several weeks after Mark returned to Calcutta, his doctor came from the mountains to visit him. Looking at all the work Mark had accomplished with the church, the school and the feeding program, the physician said, "Mark, most missionaries have spent a lifetime and not accomplished this much. No wonder you broke down!"

Seldom has Mark ever mentioned those dark days. When he had finished telling me the story, he looked at me intently and said, "I share this because if someone is discouraged, disappointed, driven, and troubled, then he must remember Jesus made a promise to never leave us nor forsake us. I have gone through the desperate fires of testing and trouble. But I can assure you that Jesus never fails; He always keeps His word."

16

Resurrection on Burial Ground Road

They've called it "Burial Ground Road" for decades, even though its real name is Park Street.

The old crowded English cemeteries are there, where the British disposed of dead men struck down by the frequent plagues of malaria.

Ironically, it was here, at an old cemetery which had been closed since 1870, that Mark Buntain decided to build his hospital.

Since embalming of the dead is not practiced in India, all bodies are completely decomposed three to four years after burial. Because of Moslem and Hindu beliefs about the dead, this land had been left untouched.

As with the school, Mark was really forced into building the massive health care unit that is now

Calcutta's newest and most beautiful facility. Stories of hospital horrors in Calcutta are legion. The Indians most often feel hospitals are places where people go to die. They cannot imagine surviving the ordeal of what passes for hospital care. Thus, the vast majority of Calcutta's sick choose to remain outside the reach of health care.

Mark learned early in his residence at Calcutta that health care would have to be part of his ministry. He knew God cared about the body as well as the soul. He also knew that historically about 25 percent of all converts in the nation of India had come to Christ through contact with hospital care. But how to accomplish this on a limited budget was beyond his imagination.

Soon after he arrived in Calcutta, Mark started a small clinic on the church compound, and then found he had to provide around-the-clock care to keep up with the needs. His tiny clinic grew, and he realized a large facility was needed.

But property was not available in Calcutta. Every vacant lot was jammed with construction, and the only spaces available were ancient cemeteries of the city. The Hindus are superstitious and they forbid anyone to build over a cemetery, even an English burial ground. So for years, he waited and prayed for some miracle.

In his jaunts of mercy through that city, Mark often passed the old English cemetery which had tombstones that had long since disappeared into dust. It was large enough for his plan, but getting the government to grant permission was another matter. And to get his missions board to approve the project was an almost impossible task. They had never approved a hospital anywhere in the world, even in the heart of deepest Africa, where the needs are also great. The Assemblies of God simply did not build hospitals. This was left to the Catholics, Adventists, and Baptists.

It is one thing to sit comfortably in America and make clear-cut decisions about such matters, and a totally different thing to live in the heart of Calcutta and see the desperate need. One day while visiting one of the government hospitals, Mark passed by the room of a dead patient. He stopped and watched as the nurse and her co-worker put intravenous needles into the corpse. Mark asked why they were doing this, since the girl had obviously been dead for several hours.

"Oh, her family will be up here pretty soon," the nurse said, "and they will want to know if we did anything to prevent the death. They will see this, and then they won't ask any questions."

Mark turned away.

Late one night an urgent call came from one of the church families. Could he rush to the government hospital? The family's married daughter had been severely burned when her clothing caught fire from a cookstove.

Mark dashed to the emergency ward and found

her lying there barely alive. No one was helping her. She had been wheeled in and left there. The staff was busy with other duties. Mark desperately tried to get the doctors to give attention to the young mother, but they let her die without care.

These incidents haunted Mark as he moved among his Indian people. They were dying and no one seemed to care. He had to do something about it. On his furloughs Mark sought permission to raise funds for a hospital. He was always flatly denied.

But God was at work nevertheless. God had moved on a group of California women about the needs of Calcutta. They started a "penny fund," and within a year they sent the money to the Foreign Missions Department for Mark to start a hospital. The board reluctantly agreed, and the Mission of Mercy Hospital project began.

Still there was the problem of property. The Indians were proficient in the game of politics. If you knew the right people, you could get remarkable things done. But Mark did not know the right people. He could not find the key to getting permission for building on Burial Ground Road.

Early one morning, while driving through the rain-soaked streets of Calcutta, Mark saw a well-dressed Indian man pressing through the soaking monsoon. He pulled over and invited the man to ride with him in the car. As they rode along, Mark mused about the need for a new hospital in Calcutta and told the stranger of his vision. The man was silent.

As Mark swung his car toward Royd Street, he looked over to a bustee area. There, crawling along on all fours like a strange insect, was a tiny boy. Mark forgot the stranger who was with him, slammed on the brakes, and jumped out into the rain. The man followed, wondering what this strange sahib was doing.

Mark bent over the boy and spoke a few words to him. Then he picked up the drenched child and disappeared into the bustee area.

"Hey! Where are you going?" the stranger called after him.

"I'm looking for this boy's mother," Mark called back over his shoulder. "I will take him to my clinic. We have a surgeon, and this child can be made to walk!"

Within a few minutes Mark returned to his car with the dirty child. They drove on, and Mark stopped by the clinic to drop off the child and give instructions to the nurses. He then returned and took the stranger to his destination.

Within a few days Mark received notification that he could have the Park Road property on a ninety-nine-year lease. The only condition was that he could not remove any soil from the grounds, since the souls of the dead were a part of the soil, according to Hindu custom.

Mark was amazed by the sudden turn of events. But then he learned the man he had picked up in the rain was the one official who held the key to releasing the Park Road property.

Next came a design for the building itself. To Mark's dismay, he discovered it would cost at least one million dollars to construct a six-story, full-service general hospital with outpatient facilities. One million dollars is a lot of money for a missionary.

"Lord, if it's all right to spend a million dollars for you in America," Mark prayed, "why can't I spend a million dollars for you in Calcutta? Jesus, I'm going to believe you for a million dollars to build this hospital right in downtown Calcutta!"

Instantly, a Scripture—Psalm 37:4—flashed through Mark's mind: "Delight thyself also in the Lord; and he shall give thee the desires of thine heart."

With that promise, he began excavation.

Calcutta is only twelve feet above sea level, and the foundation called for a depth of eighteen feet. One morning, as Mark prayed about water seeping into the foundation, he took a small Bible from his pocket, put it inside a tiny casket made of brick, laid it down on the foundation, and covered it with cement.

"Lord, we're building this hospital on your Word and for your glory," he prayed. And within minutes the water dried up—another astonishing miracle, testifying of God's love for the dying souls of India.

Money was raised, and slowly but surely the

magnificent hospital rose out of the dust of people who had lived and died before its time. Today it stands complete, as a testimony of God's love to a needy people.

And the miracles did not stop with its building. God began to bring people into Mark's life who would furnish the hundreds of thousands of dollars worth of equipment needed to run a major hospital.

Jim Bakker's concern is of special significance. Bakker is president of the nationwide, daily PTL-TV program. He has arranged for Mark to be on his program a number of times, giving the needs in Calcutta much valuable exposure. PTL's generous financial grants are of major importance and they have enabled completion of the nursing school in Calcutta. Pathology equipment was also provided by the PTL Club. They also donated two ambulances. World Vision provided other much needed equipment. The Children's Relief Fund pitched in to help. The government of Alberta, Canada, gave $100,000 to put a closed-circuit television system in the Calcutta Hospital. Most of the channels show programs on hygiene and health, but one channel is used exclusively to share the gospel of Jesus Christ. Another donor gave a mobile hospital so the Calcutta Mission of Mercy can be carried back into the bustee areas.

A Houston, Texas, man donated some of the most sophisticated physiotherapy equipment known to science, all shipped postpaid. Hospital cots came from Sweden to take up the slack until beds could be obtained.

The Rex Humbard ministry paid for enough hospital beds to furnish the entire hospital, and is paying all the shipping expense of sending these beds to Calcutta.

The hospital that started on a shoestring just a few years ago now has some of the most modern equipment in the industry. Because of this equipment, Mark has been able to attract some of India's leading medical specialists to his hospital.

Although there are many stories of great miracles concerning the hospital, perhaps just one will explain how prayer and faith have brought this about.

My wife and I invited a few close friends to our home for an evening of prayer and Bible study. Since we had just begun moving into that new home, it was a combination housewarming and thanks-for-caring evening.

After enjoying a time of fellowship, we began to share prayer requests. "I don't know how God is going to arrange it," I told the group during this time, "but I feel that within the next year I will be divinely subpoenaed to India."

The group prayed that God would reveal more about the trip. We talked about making it a church missionary project, with possibly several members of the church making the trip with us. At that time I was associate pastor with Rex Humbard at the

Cathedral of Tomorrow in Akron, Ohio.

When they left at the end of the evening, many dismissed my words from their minds. But the flame that had begun to burn in my heart for India had been strengthened by the prayers of others and the promise of God's Word.

Years before, God had sparked a flame of interest in India in my heart when Dr. Mark Buntain had been my guest speaker in a previous pastorate. Then, the friendship was renewed when Mark and I were scheduled for PTL Club guest appearances on the same day. At that time, I talked with Mark about his work in India and his hospital in Calcutta and I invited him to speak at the cathedral.

While he was at the Cathedral of Tomorrow, Mark's compassion touched deep in the heart of the church. The church presented Mark with a gift of over $6,000 for the educational, feeding, and medical programs he is operating in Calcutta.

While Mark was in town, I asked him to be a guest on my "Rejoice" radio broadcast. We were presenting a series of programs on the subject of divine healing at the time. Dr. Al Holderness, my surgeon friend, who is a Sunday school teacher at the cathedral, was also a guest on the program. Al shares Mark's fervent dedication for helping the crippled walk again. Through the power of God, Al has seen many miracles performed in the lives of his patients.

As Mark listened to Al talk about healing on the radio program, he began to worship the Lord.

"Praise Jesus!" he whispered over and over in a corner of the studio. The words were spoken in thanksgiving to our Lord—and in awe of the miracles God was performing through Al's surgical practice.

"Thank you, Jesus!" Mark prayed. The burning compassion Mark felt for India made him want to take this doctor to Calcutta for a time of sharing God's love and words of encouragement with his staff.

When the taping was over, Mark came to me privately.

"Might it be possible to have Al come to India to minister to my doctors?" Mark asked.

Something in my spirit went "click." I just knew God would work it all out.

"Yes," I told him.

Before he left Akron, Mark asked Al for advice. Would he look at the equipment list Mark's surgeons had sent to the United States with him? They had written up their needs as they saw them, and Mark wanted Al to help him decide which were basic necessities. He could not go back to his beloved India without at least the minimum requirements.

After Mark left Akron and went on to other parts of the United States, Al looked over the list of medical equipment. He sorted out the bare necessities for children's spinal surgery and came up with a minimum figure of $15,000.

Al decided to check with local representatives of

orthopedic supply companies and try to get a price discount for the Calcutta hospital. He got nowhere. Never one to be limited in his faith, Al decided to write directly to the president of one supply company and ask him to *donate* the instruments to the hospital in Calcutta.

Al was asking a lot, on behalf of people who couldn't ask for themselves. He, too, was beginning to feel the spark of compassion for India growing in his heart.

But moreover, Al had asked for the supplies because it was God's time to ask.

Now he was waiting. For almost three weeks, no answer came from the equipment supplier. During the Thursday morning men's prayer breakfast at the cathedral that week, Al asked me and the other men in attendance to agree with him in prayer that God would move on the company executives' hearts for the hospital needs. The group prayed and believed God for a miracle.

Four days later, the call came while Al was performing surgery. His assistant, Warren Neely, took the call. The Zimmer Corporation would provide $15,000 worth of spinal surgery supplies free of charge, and would replace them as they were used up.

Shortly thereafter, the materials began arriving in Al's office, and before long they were on their way to Calcutta—where a grateful staff of Indian doctors and their beloved Mark praised the Lord as they put their new supplies to use. It was a start.

Another instrument company, the DePuy Company of Warsaw, Indiana, was interested, but they wanted to talk about the project before they made a donation of materials. Al asked his associate, Warren, to present the project to them. DePuy would pay airfare for one of their Ohio salesmen, Dan Freeman, to go along if Warren would fly to Indiana to meet with company executives.

Christian Life magazine had just made the Mark Buntain story its cover story, so I gave copies of the article to Warren for himself and the salesman as he prepared for his trip to Indiana. Warren was excited about the project, but he really knew little about Mark's work. Together, Warren and I prayed that the Holy Spirit would soften the hearts of DePuy executives toward India's needs.

The plane was packed when Warren and Dan boarded for Warsaw, so they had to sit in different rows. Warren began reading the *Christian Life* article as soon as they were airborne, and the man next to him noticed what he was reading.

"Do you know that man?" he asked Warren, pointing to Mark's picture.

"No," replied Warren, "I have only talked to him briefly by phone a couple of times."

"I have known Mark Buntain for many years," the man said. "I helped him build his hospital."

For the entire flight, that man shared with Warren what God was doing through Mark Buntain in India. By the time the plane landed, Warren was glowing with victory—fully prepared to face the corporate giants.

Meanwhile, on the same flight, DePuy salesman, Dan Freeman, also began reading the magazine article. Dan was somewhat skeptical about the project. Then the man seated next to him asked, "Do you know the man in that article?"

Dan said he didn't know Dr. Buntain.

The man proceeded to explain that he was a pastor whose church had supported Mark Buntain's ministry for years. The pastor was, in fact, scheduled to leave soon for India himself, to start a church there. Before the short trip ended, Dan was thinking of ways he could help with the Buntain work in India.

Warren didn't expect to present the India project in a bar, but that's where the DePuy executive took him. He was even less prepared to hear what the man really wanted to talk about.

"Warren, I think God must be directing me to become a Christian!"

The noisy bar seemed to fall silent as the man began his story.

"My wife started going to something called 'Aglow.' Then I started running into Christians every time I turned around.

"And when I got the letter from Dr. Holderness—with a dove and a cross letterhead—I thought, 'Maybe these guys do have the answer.'"

Before Warren left Warsaw, he had an opportunity to share Christ with the busy executive. A week later, the man accepted Christ as his Savior.

The resistance Warren expected never occurred. DePuy personnel gave him a tour of the facilities and gave him a history of their firm. In 1895, Mr. DePuy had a dream of making his firm a missionary organization by supplying surgical equipment to meet medical needs around the world. As Warren listened to the story, it was apparent that this Christian man's dream was coming true three generations after it began.

The corporation executives finally asked Warren the key question: "Just what is it that you need for the Indian hospital?" Warren said he at least needed instruments for back and hip surgery.

The leadership of DePuy met privately for twenty minutes and came back with a list of materials they proposed to donate to India: instruments and related supplies for hip surgery, instruments and related supplies for the back, instruments and related supplies for the knees, equipment for traction, an external fixation device, braces and other "soft goods," equipment for treatment of scoliosis—in all, over $15,000 in equipment and supplies. The company has continued to give additional equipment since then—over $30,000 worth to date!

Warren went home praising God for the work He had started in Mr. DePuy over eighty years ago.

Before long, DePuy's personnel office called Al's

office in Akron to ask a favor. Could each of their 350 employees have a copy of the book *The Compassionate Touch* about Mark Buntain's work in India? The entire work force of the corporation had taken a personal interest in the project, and they wanted to know more about the ministry that was helping them fulfill their founder's original vision.

There appeared to be only one delay. The DePuy Company needed to know the size of Mark's orthopedic beds so they could provide the proper-sized traction equipment. They called Al, who in turn called Mark's state-side representative, Joe Ellis, in Tacoma, Washington. Joe replied that Mark had no orthopedic beds!

Al's secretary, Eleanor Bertschi, knew from the beginning that something extraordinary was going on.

"I see the hand of God in this," she said solemnly to Al one day. "How much would a new orthopedic bed cost?"

Al told her the cost was about $315, and Eleanor offered to purchase one of them to get the project going.

But God had already been moving to spread the fire of His love. Warren discovered that one of his cousins was a purchasing agent for a local hospital. He called him to ask about used orthopedic beds.

"How many do you need?" his cousin asked.

Warren threw caution to the wind and replied, "We need one hundred beds."

"Well," his cousin replied, "it just happens that I have about one hundred and fifty beds available this fall at a reasonable price." Later, Warren found out that Joel Fanberg, a member of the cathedral, works for the hospital and would be in charge of storing the beds until they could be shipped to India.

Then Warren went to see George DiFeo, a Ford dealer in North Canton, Ohio, and stated bluntly to him, "George, I need $1,000!"

"Why?" the Christian business executive automatically asked.

Warren outlined the India project to George, and immediately the Canton automobile dealer wrote out a check for $1,000.

"Just ten minutes ahead of you," he told Warren, "a check for $1,000 came to me because of a sales contest we won. My wife and I joined together in prayer when the money arrived, because we knew it was a gift of God. We knew it should be used for His work, but we didn't know where to give it.

"Then ten minutes later, Warren, you walked in to tell me about India. When you began to speak, I knew why God had sent you."

The tiny flame that began in Mark Buntain's heart twenty-five years ago had grown into a flaming desire among dozens of Americans to help the people Mark so deeply loved in India. And now God is kindling flames in the hearts of others who could help bring God's healing touch to that land.

The spark began in the heart of Al Holderness

and quickly spread to the men who attended the men's prayer breakfast at the cathedral. Those men gave many hundreds of dollars toward air fare for Al's trip to India.

Many others have given gifts of all sizes. The Sunday school classes in the children's department of the cathedral brought in jars of all sizes and shapes, collecting whatever extra change the children could bring to Sunday school to give to the starving children of India. They wanted to help.

None of this has come about as the result of a high-powered promotional campaign, because there has been none. God, in His sovereign will and wisdom, has touched the hearts of people across our continent and left one word written there: India. The hospital on Park Street stands as a great symbol of God's love and His people's concern. And all the staff wear specially designed badges that proudly proclaim, "Jesus heals." It could well be added, "Jesus cares."

17

Mark's Other Family

"Huldah could run General Motors," Mark says affectionately.

And he is probably correct. Without that expertise, Mark could never have accomplished what he has in India. Huldah oversees the bustling Buntain household with a no-nonsense efficiency. It is Huldah who serves as comptroller for the massive ministry employing over five hundred Indians. She keeps the complicated government forms flowing in proper channels and supervises all the services of the Mission of Mercy.

At any given meal, from fifteen to twenty-five people have their feet under Mark and Huldah's private table. Every nook and cranny of their small apartment is filled with people. These represent

Mark's other family.

Not that the apartment is all that plush. Mark and Huldah live in the same rooms they rented when they came to Calcutta a quarter-century ago. It is a walk-up, third-story apartment sitting over the smelly and festering city. A leper lives on their doorstep. Mark lets him stay there because there is no other place for the man to go. The leper is not alone. Probably a hundred others live on the open streets in the area of Mark's place.

Only in the last couple of years have the Buntains had running water in their apartment. However, most of the time the water for washing and cleaning has to be carted up the three floors to their apartment, since the system frequently breaks down. Furniture is adequate though antiquated, and the only thing about the apartment which seems pretentious is a large collection of finely polished brass. Not long ago a visiting American saw the collection, worth thousands of dollars in the Western world, and wondered how the missionary could afford it. What he did not know is that each piece is a loving gift from some Indian who has been touched by the life and ministry of the Buntains. These poor can't give Mark and Huldah money, but brass is common in India. So they barter for a piece of brass—or make a piece themselves—to show their love to the sahib and memsahib.

The Buntain apartment is swelteringly hot during the tropical summers and musty and wet during the monsoons. No fancy air conditioning is available for the Buntains. Almost every day the electricity breaks down and remains off for several hours. Most usually it occurs during the hot afternoons, when the still air adds to their misery. However, for the Buntains it is home, and Huldah makes sure it stays spotless. Nothing irritates her more than to see a speck of dust. Needless to say, keeping anything clean in the polluted city of Calcutta is a monumental task.

Bonnie, the Buntain's only daughter, is back in America. She works as head nurse in the intensive care unit of a large Missouri hospital, helping her husband finished his M.D. He had already received a doctorate in biochemistry, and as soon as he completes his medical degree, Jim and Bonnie will return to Calcutta to work in Mark's hospital.

Mark and Huldah have been parents to many children during their stay in India. Although they try to keep their home private, the needs are so great. Invariably either Mark or Huldah will bring a baby home sometime during the week and add to the bulging household. Lorissa is just one example.

No one really knows much about Lorissa's parents except that her mother was a prostitute. When the beautiful brown baby was born, her mother took her to Mother Teresa's Sisters of Mercy and told them she did not want the child. The sisters were soon able to find a couple to adopt the abandoned baby.

Lorissa's new father was an American black

seaman who had wandered the world and finally settled in Calcutta. There he had met an Anglo-Indian woman, and they married. The woman was ill with tuberculosis and could not bear children, so the new couple adopted Lorissa from the Sisters of Mercy.

After a couple of years the father announced he would leave for America to find work and then bring his little family over to the home of his birth. It would take some time, but he promised not to forget them. Lorissa's adopted mother feared things would never work out as they had planned. She was right. Before she and Lorissa could come to America she received a cable saying her husband had been struck down by a massive cerebral hemorrhage. He died before they could get him to the hospital.

Clutching the cable in her frail hands, Lorissa's mother took the child to Royd Street. Someone had told her the sahib would help her. Lorissa was now old enough to start school, but there was no money to pay her way.

Mark was not available when Lorissa and her adopted mother arrived. Huldah looked into Lorissa's deep eyes and felt drawn to her. Yes, they would let Lorissa attend school, and no, it would not cost anything. The mother left feeling very happy.

Just days later Huldah looked up from her desk to find Lorissa standing between two Moslem women with a bewildered look on her face.

"Her mother just died, and we don't want the

child. You must take her," they said flatly.

Tears rolled down the brown cheeks of the frightened child.

Huldah sighed and took Lorissa home. There would be another mouth to feed. Their already overstretched budget would have to stretch some more. But they could not let the little one die. Lorissa became one of Mark and Huldah's "other family."

Halfway around the globe, an Illinois family had been deep in prayer. Mrs. Manning knew God had something more for her and her husband to do. They already had two children who were extensively involved in the Lord's work. But in prayer God impressed upon them that they should adopt an Indian girl.

If the Mannings had known how virtually impossible it is to adopt such a child, they might have given up. But in simple faith, they wanted to obey God. He would help them find the child He had for them.

The Mannings didn't even know how to start looking for an answer to their prayers. When they talked to their friends, they were told to forget this desire: "If you're set on adoption, why don't you get an American baby? There are plenty of needs right here." But God had spoken, and the Mannings would listen to Him.

Months passed. One day the Mannings saw an ad in the newspaper that said Mark Buntain was slated to speak at a local church. They had never heard of this missionary, but he was from India and they wanted to meet him.

They were drawn to Mark as soon as he began to speak, and after the service they sought him out. When they spoke to him about what God had impressed on them, Mark knew immediately that Lorissa was the answer.

Maneuvering through the maze of Indian legal paperwork was not easy for Mark or the Mannings. But it was done, and today Lorissa is the legally adopted daughter of that beautiful American family. Recently she appeared as a surprise guest on a national television program which was featuring Mark. The tears flowed freely as Mark and Lorissa sat cuddled together and Mark shared the love of Christ for lost children.

When Lorissa left the Buntain household, Mark and Huldah felt a great void. But within weeks another little girl came into their lives. Maureen is an Anglo-Indian. As a young woman, Maureen's mother worked in the tea gardens of the Himalayas, and there her life had spun out of control. She lived through the years of tragedy, and Maureen was the last child of her broken life. The Buntains have adopted Maureen, and she has won their love and hearts.

There have been others, and there will be more. The Buntains are never alone. There are too many needy and hungry people for them to enjoy private dinner parties.

Mark and Huldah also have had a deep influence in the lives of their servants. Because of high unemployment, many Calcutta households have servants. In that Hindu society there is even a caste for servants, and they normally live their whole lives in a small anteroom of the apartments where they work. So Mark and Huldah inherited their household workers.

Years ago an Anglo-Indian family lived in the apartment building. As a wedding gift, their prosperous parents had given the Baileys a young Hindu servant boy named Anna. The Baileys moved to Rangoon and took Anna with them. He was a faithful servant and had great affection for the Baileys.

Then the devastation of World War II began. Fleeing from the Japanese, the Baileys abandoned their household goods and servants in Rangoon, hoping to make it to a sanctuary before being murdered by alien forces. They made it to Calcutta, but found the Japanese bombing the city, so they fled again to the northern mountains. There the Baileys settled in to escape the war and try to endure until the madness was over.

Anna, along with thousands of other servants, was left behind to face the fierce wrath of the invading armies. Thousands of servants were slain mercilessly, but Anna and a group of others managed to escape. They walked thousands of miles through India, over the frozen mountains and blasting plains. History recorded this as the "Darjeeling Trek," and hundreds of these unfortunate servants did not make it. Struck down by malaria, cholera, and dysentery, the sick were left behind to the bloody sword of the Japanese pursuers.

Anna was one of the lucky ones. He finally arrived in Calcutta—battered and bleeding, but alive.

For days Anna looked for the Baileys, and at last he learned they had fled to the mountains. Anna refused to stop until he found his masters. To their utter amazement and joy, Anna showed up to be reconciled with his employers. Loyalty between the Baileys and Anna went very deep. After the war the Baileys moved back to Calcutta and took an apartment. They brought Anna and his new wife with them.

Sometime later the Baileys were transferred out of India. They could not take their servants with them. Anna and his wife, Yakama, now had two children. In addition, Anna's nephew had joined the servants' household. When the Baileys left, they asked the Buntains to take Anna and his family.

Mark detests the caste system, and he immediately improved the lot of Anna's family. He gave them better quarters, and as the children grew, they formed fast friendships with the Buntains. Later Mark and Huldah took the servant children into their own home and raised them as their own.

This love had a deep impact on Anna and his family, even though they could not understand the strange ways of the white man. They knew something was different about him and his wife.

The turning point came when Mark had given one of the servant children a new watch. The boy was so proud and carefully guarded it. But the newness inevitably wore off and he became careless. One day, while playing ball, Krishna took the watch off and laid it down. While he was busy enjoying the game, someone stole the watch.

When Krishna discovered the theft, fear gripped his heart. He knew the sahib was kind, but all servants expect beatings—or at least bitter verbal abuse—for their mistakes. That night Krishna would not go home. Bonnie found him outside crying.

At dinner she told her dad what had happened. Mark knew this was the time to show his servants the love of Jesus.

Mark said nothing to anyone. The next day he went to the store and bought an even more beautiful watch for Krishna. That night Mark called the boy in.

"Krishna," he said, "did you lose your watch?"

"Yes, sahib," he said, fear clouding his dark eyes.

Mark handed him the package. "Krishna, I'm sorry you lost your watch," Mark said to him, "but I have bought a better one for you. This is yours. Go now, and remember we love you."

The boy raced out of Mark's presence hardly

believing his ears. He ran to his dad's room and told him what happened. The old man shook his head and said, "I can't understand it. This must be Christianity."

Shortly afterward, Mark noticed Anna had started reading a native Bible. Krishna and his sister began attending Mark's church, and both were saved. Anna and his wife came that night as their children were baptized. Before long Anna and Yakama gave their hearts to Christ and were also baptized. Today they are strong members of Mark's church, loving the Lord whom they first met in the lives of the Buntains. Krishna now works for Mark's ministry as an accountant for the school.

On another hot India day, Huldah looked up from her desk to see a mother standing in front of her with a curly-headed, ten-year-old son.

"Will you please help us?" the mother pleaded. "The Catholic school has closed, and now my little Faiz has no school to attend." The mother quickly went on. "He shows such great promise, but he has no school to go to."

The little boy smiled at Huldah and his big, brown eyes twinkled. She wanted to help, but what could she do? The school was already overcrowded, the funds depleted. There was a waiting list several hundred names long of people who desired enrollment. They simply did not have room for the little boy.

Huldah had almost told the pleading mother she

could not help when suddenly from deep within she felt they should take this little fellow into the program.

Then she began to question herself.

"Where will we get the money for his support? What will the teachers say when I bring another child into a class already filled beyond capacity?"

But somehow Huldah knew God would take care of all the problems. She had to help little Faiz.

Faiz studied hard and did very well in school. He was first in his class each year, and in his final year in high school he was elected associated student body president.

Faiz listened year after year to the presentation of the gospel in the chapel services. Coming from a Moslem home, he found the lessons somewhat strange. But in 1968, while attending a youth camp sponsored by Mark's church, Faiz accepted Christ as his personal Savior. Here is how it happened.

The boy had been given an ancient wrist watch by his Moslem father. At the camp, someone slipped into his room and stole it. Faiz was shattered, and he told the camp counselors. After a careful search, it was obvious no one from the camp was responsible for the theft. The wrist watch must have been taken by some of the children who lived in a nearby village.

That night Faiz attended the camp service. For the first time he went to the altar to pray. "Jesus, if you are the Son of God," he said, "help me to find my watch. If you do, I will then know you are the only true God."

The next day one of the camp counselors had to go to town for supplies. When she arrived, the store did not have the needed supplies, and she was told a place in the next village would help her.

When the counselor arrived at the new village and got into the marketplace, one of the old men asked her, "Has anyone in your camp lost a wrist watch? One of our village boys stole a watch and we found it. Here, we want to give it back to you."

Faiz was overjoyed. And, faithful to his word, he went to the altar that night and gave his heart to Christ. In the words of Faiz, "The candle of my life was lit." His life took on new meaning and purpose. He had found true peace.

Soon afterward he felt God had called him into a full-time ministry to his own people. Immediately Faiz made plans to further this call. A sponsor, Mrs. Clarence Horne, who lived in Georgia, was contacted. She was willing to sponsor Faiz in college, and she enabled him to come to the United States.

The late Dr. C.C. Burnett, former President of Bethany Bible College, Santa Cruz, California, had visited Calcutta. While he was there he made an indelible impression on Faiz. Young Faiz, sure of a call to preach, applied to the college for enrollment.

In the spring of 1976, Faiz graduated with honors from the college. In his senior year he was president of the student body, the first foreign student ever to achieve that position.

During Christmas of 1976, the student body at Bethany took up a love offering to send Faiz back to Calcutta for a visit. He would return to the United States to attend seminary before going back permanently to Calcutta, to work with Mark and Huldah. When Faiz walked off the plane in Calcutta, the whole church was there. Mark and Huldah glowed with pride.

But the story was not over yet. During these years in Calcutta, another young person was seeking God for His will in her life. Joy David was the church pianist at Royd Street. She had earned both her B.A. and B.Ed. in music at the local university and had begun teaching at the church day school. Besides winning many local music awards, Joy had won the All-India Youth for Christ award for the top keyboard solo, as well as the piano teacher's Challenge Cup in Music Theory from London.

In spite of her accomplishments and her beauty, Joy was in despair. She was almost twenty-three years old and unmarried, and her parents had already begun arrangements for her to marry a young doctor in a small city in South India. Parent-arranged marriages are still common in India, but it was difficult for Joy. Her heart's desire was to be actively involved in full-time Christian ministry.

During this time, Joy attended a youth camp.

Without knowing what was troubling her, the speaker said, "Remember, you must seek first the kingdom of God and His righteousness, and then the other things will be taken care of." Joy took God at His word.

About this time, Mark was facing problems caused by the rapid growth of his Teen Challenge work. About fourteen boys lived in the mission compound, and the facilities were far from adequate. Rats kept getting into their clothing. Another house with three or four large bedrooms and a large living room was needed.

Mark placed an ad in the newspaper, and got one response. A man had bought a house several years ago for $43,750 and the real estate agent had assured him he could now sell it for $62,500. But after Mark told him what the house was to be used for, the owner agreed to sell it to the Calcutta church for his original investment of $43,750.

Mark agreed to buy the house, although he didn't know where the money would come from. He would have to pay $6,250 down and the balance in installments.

Most of Mark's mission funds had gone into the new hospital. There was only one thing to do. He must appeal to the people of the Assemblies of God churches. But he felt dissatisfied with this.

"Why must I always go to America with my hands out?" Mark said to his people the next Sunday. "I know you are very poor people, but I feel God wants us to take on this project."

At the end of the service, Associate Pastor Ron Shaw stepped to the pulpit to give the benediction. Instead of dismissing the service, Shaw, with tears in his eyes, told the congregation he wanted to give the money he had been saving for a television set (a station recently had begun broadcasting in Calcutta) toward the Teen Challenge Center.

What followed from that congregation was a sacrifice of love which would be hard to equal.

"People gave their rings," an observer noted. "Ladies took off their gold jewelry (gold is a symbol of virtue in India). A dozen watches were laid on the platform."

Joy saw the sacrificial giving of those people. The next week she went to her bank to withdraw some money for the Teen Challenge project. The words of the youth camp speaker haunted her: "Seek ye first the kingdom of God."

"Lord, I wonder what it would be like," she prayed, "to give you everything I have just once. I may never be able to do this again."

Instead of withdrawing only the amount she had intended, Joy closed her account. Living at home and teaching full-time, she had been able to save almost all her small earnings over the past nine months. When Joy gave the money to Mark, he said to her, "You don't know what this must mean to God, Joy. He'll pay you back a hundredfold for what you've done."

Far away in America, Faiz knew nothing of Joy's personal struggle to accept the marriage her family was planning. He had known Joy casually when he was in school in Calcutta, but now returning to India he seemed drawn to her.

"It was love at second sight," he admits.

That same week he took her on their first date.

From that time on, it was a rare thing to see Faiz and Joy apart. By the time of the church's big Christmas program, they were ready to announce their engagement. Joy's parent-arranged marriage had been cancelled. God's plan included something better for a girl who was willing to give Him her all.

Only three days into 1977, Faiz and Joy were married. The pews were crowded in the Royd Street church as they exchanged their vows. Pastor Mark officiated. The church was overjoyed at the faithfulness of a loving and caring God.

During Mark's last furlough in the States, Faiz and Joy joined him for a service in San Jose. Mark told their story and presented the couple to the California congregation. It was an inspired and moving moment.

Later, standing in the parking lot, Mark put his arms around Faiz and Joy and said, "Joy, your friends and even your brothers have dreamed all their lives of coming to America to school. They never made it. But look what Jesus has done for you, because you gave your all."

Since then, Faiz has completed his Master of

Religious Education degree at Golden Gate Theological Seminary in Mill Valley, California. And Joy has taken several graduate courses in music. Many students who come to the United States from India never go back, but Faiz and Joy have returned to join the staff of the church and school in Calcutta.

18

An Indian Grave

"How can you call yourself a missionary and be so prejudiced?" Mark's hand trembled as he clutched the fragile blue tissue letter from half a world away. He was no stranger to biting criticism, but this was a deeper hurt than he had ever known. His own blood daughter, the beautiful and tender Bonnie, had penned the poison words that stung and stunned.

Mark slumped down in his swivel office chair and tried to blink away the tears. Happy cries from his playing schoolchildren drifted in unheard as he sat in the darkness of his windowless office. He was unaware of anything except his own sorrow. The heaviness in his chest was almost physical. He reread the short, angry note, but still the words would not go away.

"Where have I gone wrong, God," Mark whispered hoarsely into the darkness. "Why have I lost her?"

The question was not easily answered since the roots of the poisoned tree were from seeds planted two years before.

Bonnie had blossomed into a beautiful young woman. She stood tall and her fair skin was in deep contrast to the dark faces of her playmates and friends. Mark and Huldah had always worried about the day when their daughter would want to leave them to form her own family. Tragedy, hardship, love and laughter had cemented the little family together. Although there were always other children who lived in the home and shared in the deep family love, Bonnie was still their very own daughter. She was a Buntain, born of the same Scottish-English stock of her fiercely loyal and loving ancestors.

Now an outsider was threatening all of this.

The outsider was a handsome Indian boy. He was a member of Mark's church and came from a good Christian family. He was proud to date the missionary's daughter and before long a deep attachment had grown between Bonnie and her new friend. It was never love, but Mark feared it might become that and he objected to the arrangement.

It was not that the youth was Indian, but that he manipulated the emotions of their daughter that disturbed Mark so much. But Bonnie could not see this. She believed the antagonists around her who called her parents' opposition "racial prejudice." A rift developed in the family; it was small at first, but each day the strain forced the crack to widen. The tension was becoming unbearable.

The problem was compounded by the moodiness of Bonnie's friend, and her peers who pointed to "prejudice." The strain had become critical and Mark worried long into many a sleepless night.

Today Bonnie cannot even recall writing that letter. In fact she says, "I would never do anything to hurt my father. He is almost supernatural. I can't understand how a human can love as he does, pray and walk with the Lord so closely as my daddy. I love my dad more than anything." But Mark remembers.

Bonnie was more Indian than American. She thought like an Indian. In fact Bonnie could speak four Indian dialects before she learned English. She never wanted to leave Calcutta. While other missionary children attended European schools in India, Bonnie was raised with the Indians. She preferred to sleep on the floor with the Indian children and liked their food more than the bland and tasteless American diet. She had no desire to come to America and the furloughs every four years traumatized her. Calcutta was her home. America was a foreign and strange land. Thus it was natural for her to develop a relationship with an Indian young man.

In this frame of thought it was difficult for Bonnie

to understand why Mark opposed the dating arrangement. She felt threatened by the opposition and the tension became more and more painful. Her Indian boyfriend accented the problem by playing each Buntain against the other. It was at this time that Bonnie left for college in the United States. She didn't want to go, but parental pressure and educational realities forced the decision.

When Bonnie arrived in the United States she experienced culture shock. She was lonely and angry. No one understood her and the American youth were strange to her Indian ways. She missed her family. She missed her Indian friend. It was while she was in this mood that she wrote her angry note, perhaps hoping her family would panic and call her back to Calcutta.

Mark didn't know anything to do but pray. He had been fasting and praying about the matter for two years. But now it was at the breaking point. Something had to be done. Mark buried his face in his hands and fell heavily across the desk weeping for his lonely daughter. The burden was so heavy. He felt he could not bear it. God had to do something.

God did do something although it would be months before Mark learned of it. It was not a sudden flash from the sky or a dramatic "act of God"; rather, it was a slow and gradual healing.

Jim Long entered Bonnie's life.

Actually he had already made an entrance a decade before. Jim, son of a missionary family, had first met Bonnie in Calcutta. His parents were sent to replace Mark and Huldah while the Buntains came back for their year's furlough and deputation. Jim and Bonnie struck up a friendship. But the years and circumstances of ministry had separated them for a decade. The Buntains and Longs had lost touch.

When Bonnie enrolled at Evangel College in Springfield, Missouri, her roommate turned out to be Jim Long's sister. Jim was away at medical school. He wanted to become a doctor, but Bonnie and the other Longs spent many hours together. During the difficult weeks of working through her culture shock, Jim Long's mother counseled, prayed with, and loved Bonnie, understanding the loneliness and her sense of loss. Slowly but surely the hurt healed and Calcutta receded into the past, taking with it her relationship with the Indian youth. Only Bonnie's deep love for her mother and dad remained.

As the months passed, the Indian youth decided to come to America to attend college. He realized Bonnie was slipping away from him and felt if he could be with her he could get her back. Arrangements were made and he came. Strangely, Mark made it possible for the young man to come. He said, "He had the call of God on his life and I would never stand in the way of anyone who wants to be a minister for our Lord." Mark worried about his coming, but he had to trust God.

It was different when Bonnie and the boy met half a world away. The youth tried to reach her through his moods and manipulation, but Bonnie could not be reached. It was over.

The Longs provided Bonnie with family warmth and a fond touch with her Indian past. Then Jim came home. Jim didn't take long to announce his intentions and the Buntains were informed of an impending wedding. The wedding took place in Vancouver, British Columbia, and the foreign missions board permitted Mark to fly home for a few days so he could perform the ceremony.

The story doesn't end there. In fact, in many ways it only starts here for the new generation of Buntains in India. Jim and Bonnie feel God has called them to be medical missionaries and are preparing for work in Mark's hospital. Jim will have his medical degree and also a Ph.D. in biochemistry and research. He will finish his training and plans to be in Calcutta permanently within three years. Bonnie is a registered nurse and heads the intensive care unit at a major American hospital. They plan to spend their lives in Calcutta working with Mark in the ministry God has given them. Mark feels he could never have found a better son-in-law and breaks into a wide grin when Jim's name is mentioned. Jim and Bonnie have been married three years now and live in Missouri while Jim is finishing his medical training.

Tall and attractive, the missionary's blonde daughter is noticeably ill at ease with the whirring tape recorder in front of her. "I don't want anyone else to hear this tape," she says, opening her heart to talk about the pains of the past and the hurts her daddy has known. She reluctantly shares the difficult story of her brief alienation, obviously deeply hurt that she caused her dad even the briefest moment of emotional pain. At times tears well up in her soft hazel eyes and moments later they flash with anger when she talks about those who have hurt her dad. She is intensely loyal and sometimes slips into a sadness as she talks.

"Dad will die in India," she says, "and I'm afraid he won't have much time left. He works too hard. He cares too deeply."

Bonnie reaches back to the breakdown and talks quietly about that most difficult time. She remembers when he had to beg the foreign missions board for the hospital and in the midst of that battle was struck down with severe chest pains. "Everyone thought he was having a heart attack," she says. "But I knew different. There was nothing wrong with his heart. He merely suffered from the intensity of those sessions. I sat by his hospital bedside and held his hand during those difficult days. The doctors confirmed my suspicions and released him with a warning not to care so deeply. But it has done no good."

Bonnie leans forward and narrows her eyes in anger. "I've seen him receiving letters from the States questioning his work and methods and have seen him weep because he was misunderstood."

Leaning back thoughtfully and shivering in the coolness of the air-conditioned Tacoma conference room of her uncle's church, Bonnie sighs, "He always says it. It's almost the first thing I remember him saying. He seldom talks about India without mentioning it."

"What does he say, Bonnie?" I ask.

"It's something Judson wrote about Burma. Only dad changes 'Burma' to 'India.' He says,

Only one prayer I ask.
   Only one good I crave,
To finish my task,
   And then to die within
      an Indian grave.

"He really means it," Bonnie sighs. "You know that another missionary organization asked him to leave Calcutta four years ago to help them raise missionary funds. They said he could live in America and travel all over the world preaching. He turned it down. He could not bring himself to abandon Calcutta."

"There have been other offers," I urge, hoping she will continue the warm reflection.

"Oh, yes, many. In fact one of the strangest came only recently. Another Christian leader approached dad and asked him to spend the rest of his life just praying for missions. The man offered him a fantastic lifetime salary and a large, expensive house in the

USA. He wanted dad to spend the rest of his life in prayer. He said dad would never again have to worry."

"He turned it down?"

"Of course," Bonnie adds. "Without Calcutta dad would die."

Later I learned details of this unusual offer. During the very difficult days when Bonnie had been alienated from her dad, the Christian leader somehow learned of the struggle. Bonnie and Huldah were in America while Mark remained alone in Calcutta. The man phoned Mark stating, "It's urgent that you come to America immediately. It involves your daughter." That's all he told Mark.

Mark's heart almost stopped as he received the phone call. What could be wrong? There were no details given and Mark could not reach his relatives. He immediately rushed to the security policy to try to get permission to go home. Such a request would take several days to clear even though it was an emergency.

While Mark worried and waited he received a phone call from a Calcutta hotel. To his amazement the man who had called him had flown to Calcutta and wanted to see Mark. The missionary rushed to the hotel to find what was wrong. When he arrived, the aggressive Christian leader began to apply pressure for Mark to leave Calcutta and head his prayer program.

"You owe it to your daughter," he urged. "How

can you stay in Calcutta when you are losing your only child? If you'll come to America you can be with your family and head my program."

For over two hours the man pressured, intimidated, pleaded with and almost threatened Mark in order to get him to accept the position. But Mark knew he could not leave Calcutta despite the personal pain of family troubles.

Later Mark said those were some of the darkest days of his life. The offer was so tempting, the pressure so intense. But he had to stay in Calcutta.

"What will happen when he is gone?" I ask, resuming our conversation.

"I sometimes worry about that," Bonnie muses. "There is Ron Shaw to carry on, and Faiz. Then there will be Jim and me. We all love India and want to spend our lives telling the people about Jesus. But no one has the same degree of passion that dad has for India.

"The hospital and the church will go on. The school will prosper. The Teen Challenge Center will grow. We'll continue to feed the hungry. Someone will pick up dad's correspondence teaching course, which now enrolls over 200,000 Indians. The work will go on. But no one can take dad's place."

The conversation falls silent and only the soft whirr of the tape recorder can be heard. A gentle knock interrupts our thoughts and Mark timidly peeks inside.

(It was unusual for Mark to be home. He normally

only comes to America every four years. But he had received a cable from an Alaskan pastor who pleaded for him to preach a weekend missions convention. Mark's foreign missions field director was in Calcutta when the cable came and he urged Mark to accept. He could stop by Tacoma and visit his pregnant daughter and aged mother before returning to Calcutta. Of course, Huldah would have to stay in India during the time Mark was away.)

"Pardon me," Mark shyly interrupts. "Could we just take a little break and catch a bite to eat. They're waiting for us."

Mark only has one day with his daughter and he wants to spend every moment with her. We all pile into a car to drive to a nearby restaurant. It is a typical Buntain family get-together.

Huldah is in Calcutta grappling with the intense problems of the work. Fulton is away visiting the Holy Land. Alice and Ed are traveling with Mark's new missionary film somewhere in the USA. Jim is home in Missouri struggling with medical textbooks. Only Bonnie and Mark's mother are with him. But even now time is so precious that one of Mark's Calcutta Mission of Mercy board members and his wife have joined us. After all, even at this family gathering work has to be done.

On the way to the restaurant Kathleen Buntain talks proudly of her son. "Sometimes," she says, "I sit in the church and weep with joy for how God has used Mark." Kathleen now lives in the massive and beautiful senior citizens' complex built by Fulton and his church. Now eighty-five years old, she still has her sharp wit and clear mind. She talks warmly and quietly the whole way. Mark sits in front, with his arm around Bonnie, whispering to her during their brief moment of privacy.

During the dinner Mark worries out loud about his latest problems. We try to encourage Mark, but our words are empty and we know it.

It seems he hardly knows what he is eating as he begins to talk about his beloved people. Bonnie and Kathleen are used to these verbal excursions and long ago learned not to resent his passion. Rather, they gently listen and encourage him as he shares the burdens of his heart.

The restaurant finally empties and Mark is still talking of India. He speaks warmly of Faiz and Joy, of Maureen, Ron and Felicia Shaw. He expresses concern and asks prayer for one of his Indian deacons now grappling with cancer. Mark's eyes cloud with tears. He breaks into a soft, "Thank you, Jesus; thank you, Jesus, for touching my India." It's late now and time to go.

Mark walks with his mother and daughter to the car. They all know that in just a few short hours he will again be leaving for India. Mom Buntain long ago faced the fact that she would die alone without her oldest son by her side. She knows he has to return to India. After all, Dad Buntain long ago had said, "Mark, as long as there is still one lost soul in India you have to go back."

Looking down on his pregnant daughter, Mark beams, "I'm so thrilled about the baby." God is so faithful. The Buntains will live for and love India for still another generation to come.

The trio walks slowly to the car, arms fondly wrapped around each other. Tonight was theirs. A proud mother who thrilled in this warm moment, thinking how the years of sacrifice were all worth it. A concerned daughter who fretted about her daddy's health and wished she could somehow relieve his worry. And the new baby stirring in Bonnie's womb, holding faith for the future. Three generations of Buntains—actually four generations—walking into the warmth of the spring night holding on to each other and wishing the moment could last forever.

If you desire to be part of Mark's ministry by prayer and support, his American address is:

Mark Buntain
Calcutta Mission of Mercy
1717 South Puget Sound
Tacoma, WA 98405

For free information on how to receive
the international magazine

LOGOS JOURNAL

also Book Catalog

Write: Information

LOGOS JOURNAL CATALOG
Box 191
Plainfield, NJ 07061